EARTH   AIR

ELEMENTAL MAGICK

Meditations, Exercises, Spells, and Rituals to Help You Connect With Nature

D. J. CONWAY

New Page Books
A division of the Career Press, Inc.
Franklin Lakes, NJ

ELEMENTAL MAGICK
EDITED AND TYPESET BY KATE HENCHES
Cover design by Kort Kramer
Cover art by Lisa Hunt
Printed in the U.S.A. by Book-mart Press

To order this title, please call toll-free 1-800-CAREER-1 (NJ and Canada: 201-848-0310) to order using VISA or MasterCard, or for further information on books from Career Press.

The Career Press, Inc., 3 Tice Road, PO Box 687,
Franklin Lakes, NJ 07417
www.careerpress.com
www.newpagebooks.com

Library of Congress Cataloging-in-Publication Data

Available upon request.

Contents

Chapter 4: THE ELEMENT OF WATER

Chapter 5: THE ELEMENT OF SPIRIT

Chapter 6: OTHER INTERACTIONS

IntroductioN

Magickal Building Blocks
of the Universe

Everything in the universe is created from specific building blocks or ingredients. These are called Elements. The scientific community (with its limited knowledge) agrees with this, but disagrees as to what the Elements are called, what they may or may not do, and whether there are beings associated with them. Although their names for the Elements, and the way they divide the Elements, are worded differently, both scientists and magicians are talking about exactly the same creating ingredients. The differences are only a matter of semantics.

From the beginnings of human acknowledgement and use of religion and magick, cultures knew that the four Directions of the terrestrial plane were connected with four Elements: North (Earth); East (Air); South (Fire);

and West (Water). Ceremonial magicians, Pagans, and Wiccans all correspond these Elements to the Four Quarters of the universe, the Zodiac (astrology), and any magickal circle. In most ritual ceremonies, one of the first steps is to call upon the four Elements and their rulers in their proper Direction. This invokes the Elemental Spirits to protect their Quarter of the circle against negatives of any kind.

Magicians, Pagans, and New Age followers of all paths know that there are four Elements: Earth, Air, Fire, and Water. To those who study deeply into this subject, they soon learn there is a fifth, nebulous Element called Spirit. To many of these people, there appears to be no practical purpose in learning much about the Elements, so they run through the learning process as quickly as possible, never seeing the possibilities that lie waiting. However, because of ritual use, it is vitally important to what each Element is and what it can do and not do.

Alchemists, philosophers, and magicians have recognized and used the four Elements for at least 3,000 years. Although records beyond this point are scanty or nonexistent, it is highly likely that the same knowledge was shared and used by tribal shamans, priests, and priestesses in their religious ceremonies and magick as far back as the beginning of humans living in clans.

There are a wide variety of opinions and interpretations of the Elements, each holding clues to the meanings of these esoteric materials. My opinions will differ from those of others. This doesn't make them or me wrong. It merely points out the fact that we look at the same material in different ways, many times according to how we have grown on our spiritual paths. Change should be constant. Where there is no change, there eventually becomes a vacuum. Nature, abhorring a vacuum, will fill it with something. If you want your life and spiritual path to be filled with positive experiences, take an active part in deciding what your future goals are and how you will accomplish them. You can most easily do this by working with the Elements and Elementals.

The Elements are also the magickal building blocks of everything from what we call natural events to magick. The Elements, or combinations thereof, are found in every single object, being, or happening in the entire universe. So it is in our best interests that we understand as much about them as possible.

All magick is primarily based on the four Elements. These Elements are, in reality, forces, energies, and substances— all at the same time. In magick, we combine different mixtures of the Elements on the astral plane for a specific purpose or result. When properly combined and seasoned with time, that purpose or result manifests itself on the physical plane of existence.

In this book, I will explain, according to my own understanding, about the mystical, mysterious Elements, the energies and forces that lie behind each Element, and particularly the Elemental Spirits that arise from these Elements. When I speak of Elemental Spirits, I don't mean creatures that have total existence in the world of matter. They may make temporary appearances in this plane of existence, but they are not of a physical nature. These beings, and the Elements they represent, are more a tendency than an actual product. However, the Elements themselves have certain qualities, natures, moods, and magickal purposes. Usually, they are called kingdoms and are said to have rulers. They have both positive and negative traits, which can affect humans and events on this planet, as well as the universe itself. So do the Elemental Spirits that are connected to them.

Although the Elemental Spirits are made of ethereal, spiritual material, they have a direct effect on the visible world, because of their attachment to an Element. All visible things have more than one Element in their construction. Even human personalities come under this multiple influence and are believed to reflect the pattern of the soul in their balance or imbalance of Elements.

Cultural differences sometimes changed the descriptions of some of the Elements. Physical settings, such as climate or hemisphere, could also affect the belief of an Element's power or its traits. For example, in Ireland and Scotland, the Celts knew the four Elements as the Four Airts (winds), or castles of the four winds. In Africa, the Element of Fire, which represented the sun, was an enemy. In the Southern Hemisphere, not only the seasons, but the positions of the Elements of North and South are reversed.

Working with certain Elemental Spirits is the best way to become familiar with the Element itself, how you can handle its energy, and for what purposes. Because Elemental Spirits cannot exist without the Element in which they live, one must learn something about the Elements themselves first. The Elemental beings are quite powerful and frequently work with humans on projects that interest them. They can see, hear, and feel, but have no physical organs to register these senses as humans do. However, they have the power to mold the creative forces of the Elements to produce any desired physical manifestation.

Elemental Spirits can only be perceived by "feelings" or "the inner eyes." They are rarely seen with the physical eyes. They are living beings whose ethereal world exists on a different vibration level than ours. This world interpenetrates, yet is separate from, the physical world of matter. Elemental Spirits did not evolve along the same lines as humans, and they will never become human, nor do humans become Elementals.

These ethereal beings can assume any appearance they want, but usually match the picture imprinted on the minds of those humans who are around. Every country has its fairy tales of Elemental Spirits. Some African tribes called them the Yowahoos. The ancient Egyptians and present-day Arabs called them the Afrites; to the people of India they were the Daityas. In the Jewish Kabala, they were known as the Shedim, which were then further divided into four classes.

The Elemental Spirits do not suffer sickness as we know it, but do react to violence and strong negative emotions. When they feel unappreciated or misused, it hurts them. Then they will either move out of the area of the troubling humans or cause the offending humans a great amount of trouble. They can vary in form from very tiny to gigantic, but usually contain some human likeness.

Sometimes Elemental Spirits will have a secondary nature in another Element, which will be discussed later in the book. They can cooperate and partially merge with each other, but cannot enter or control Elements other than their own. These connections of Spirits from different Elements allow the magickal energy to flow in a continuous circle around the Element of Spirit, or the Creative Void.

Frequently, statues, amulets, talismans, and sometimes specific places, will have Elemental Spirits attached to them; hence the story of the genie or Djinn of the lamp or ring. Sometimes, the attachment is temporary; at other times, it is permanent. If one is fortunate enough to own a piece of jewelry with an Elemental attached to it, treat that jewelry with love and respect. In return, you will be gifted with good luck.

Although the Elements are prominent in every area of our lives, we can positively change events by working with them instead of against them, or worse, doing nothing at all. As long as you are not using magick to harm or to control others, the use of magick to better your life is not wrong. It is no different than strong prayers in other religions.

By learning to balance the Elements with the aid of the Elemental Spirits, we can better balance our lives and personal environments, our towns, and then slowly spread this balance out to encompass the entire world and universe. We will also be presented with more and more universal phenomena, such as crop circles, to study and ponder and work at deciphering. What we now know about the Elements is only the tip of the iceberg of knowledge about these magickal building blocks. We actually know very little of the Elemental Spirits that surround us at all times. These beings are the ambassadors of the Elements to humans. Most of the remaining knowledge about these astral creatures is buried in old folk tales. To learn the truth, one must follow barely visible threads through hundreds of remaining tales, assimilate the collected data with common sense, and reach a logical conclusion.

We also find the use of Elements in astrology, where Earth, Air, Fire, and Water are considered to be fixed, cardinal, or mutable in nature. In astrological charts, we can see the Elemental Spirits at work in their effect on human personalities or life events. Lack of the influence of an Element in a personal chart will appear in life as an imbalance. This lack can be filled by specifically working with the missing Elemental Spirits who work with that missing Element. Sometimes, these Elemental Spirits will bring another person into your life whose chart contains the balancing Element needed. Other times, one must have frequent contact with the necessary Elemental Spirits, plus immersion in or nearness to the physical manifestations of the needed Element.

Besides explanations and descriptions of the Elements, there will be short meditations, exercises, spells, and rituals to help the reader learn more about the Elements and the Elemental Spirits.

When you balance the Elements within yourself, and learn how to communicate and work with the Elemental Spirits, you will find yourself in the center of the Elemental circle. And the nebulous Element of Spirit always is found in the center of the other four Elements. Being drawn into the esoteric energy of Spirit causes humans to move upward on their spiritual journey. This connection with the Element of Spirit may last only a few seconds or a few minutes, but when experienced, the human soul will always seek the purity of this higher Element.

So we constantly work with and walk the path of the four Elements with our soul-eyes on the Element of Spirit. We learn that the more we know of the other Elements and their Elementals, the more will be revealed whenever we make that momentary connection with Spirit.

How to Use This Book

The Power Animals listed in the Characteristic Tables are energies to call upon during spellwork or rituals. The term "dark" does not mean evil. It means "more aggressive, protective, and a type of energy to balance those of light." These animals can also be called upon for shapeshifting, especially for shamans. The bear and turtle are light energies that represent the positive side of the Earth Element, while the wolf and lynx are the balancing negative energies of Earth. The dark energies have a heavier, very different feel to them, energies that are often needed to push things back into balance when they have swung too far in one direction.

The Element table given in each appropriate chapter is based on traditional beliefs, unless otherwise stated. By studying the characteristic tables for each Element, you will find it easier to plan rituals and spells, and to reach a spiritual understanding of each Element and its Elemental Spirits. To strengthen your contact with the proper Spirits, use as many symbols as you feel necessary when you perform a ritual, spell, or meditation. Even visualizing these symbols will aid you in your contacts and desired manifestations.

For meditations and Otherworld journeys, you can use the same symbols in reality or visualization. This way you can experience more detailed meetings with the Elemental Spirits. Also watch for certain symbols in your dreams and meditations. Through these symbols you will know when the Elementals send messages to you.

Now, let us begin our journey....

THE ELEMENT OF EartH

Like Earth, be balanced with a
solid foundation.

The Element of Earth is solid, dense matter, a tangible material that can be touched and felt by humans in this physical world. It is also anything that has a solid form in the Otherworld or astral plane. In the Welsh language, the term for Earth is *Calas*, which means everything hard or firm in structure. The Earth Element represents the final stages of creation or magick, for all manifestations are first formed in the astral world, and then must appear in the physical world, or the Element of Earth. This applies even if the magickal result is love, healing, creative ideas, or prosperity.

In modern Paganism and Wicca, rituals and magick are performed in a sacred space that is created by magickally casting an invisible circle. This circle becomes a space between the worlds—for a time a sacred spot that has access to this world and the Otherworld. Within this circle, a dark green candle, and any other symbols representing Earth, is placed just inside the North side. In the Southern Hemisphere, the Earth Element is considered to be in the South. This placement is one of the four quarters, with the altar in the center representing Spirit.

The Element of Earth influences human personalities by imparting a sense of balance and solidity in life. We can be out of balance if we have little or no Earth in a natal chart. We can also suffer imbalance if we do not keep in touch with nature on a regular basis. If we become aware of such an imbalance, we need to make a conscious effort to realign the Elements within our psychic bodies. This may take the form of spending more time in nature, or by deliberately cultivating or renewing relationships with Earth Elementals. These are discussed on pages 22-39. At other times, we feel an imbalance of an Element because we have used up that Element's energy just in the process of living our daily stressful lives. The same techniques mentioned previously are used to rebalance in this event.

Every culture on this planet, at some point in their development, knew of and used the energies of the Elements. The names, colors, and descriptions were sometimes different from those we recognize today, but the underlying basics were the same. For example, the Irish believed there were four chief winds and eight subordinate winds. Their descriptions of the four chief winds fit the four Elements.

To the Celts in general, the four Directions or Elements were Wind Castles. However, in Scotland, they were called the Airts, which means airs or winds. The Northern Castle of the Winds was colored black. All of these "Castles" were guarded by the Great Goddess and were the keys to the Underworld. The Northern Castle was associated with the Earth.

In Norse mythology, the god Odin gave four dwarves the eternal task of holding up the sky. No colors are listed for the directions. In the North, the dwarf Nordhri ruled ice, or the Earth Element.

There were several versions of the Elements among the Native Americans, depending upon the tribe and the writer. One is that the North was white and associated with the buffalo. To the Navajo and the Cheyenne, the North was black, while to the Zuni the North and the Earth Element was white. Other tribes did not list colors, but knew the Elements only as Spirit Keepers. To one such clan, the North was known as Waboose.

The ancient Mayans believed that four deities called Bacabs held up the sky with the aid of trees. The Northern direction was considered to be the color black.

Other cultures in ancient Mexico believed that different colors corresponded to the directions and Elements. To them, the North was the Fire Element, colored red.

The Tattwas symbols from India are excellent to use for visualization of the Elements. These geometric designs of the magickal Elements are plain, unadorned, basic, and primitive, with a deep meaning to the subconscious mind. They can be used separately or together. The symbol for the Earth Element and the North is a yellow square.

China had more than one designation of the directions. One system given, without correspondence to the directions, says that the four cardinal points were associated with the Black Warrior, White Tiger, Vermillion Bird, and Azure Dragon. The Four Hidden Dragons of Wisdom, however, was said to be the center and the gateway to Spirit. In another system, the Chinese said that the Element of Earth was the center; it was colored yellow.

During the Middle Ages in Europe and parts of the Mediterranean, there arose two types of ceremonial magicians known as Enochian and Kabalistic. Later, these beliefs were incorporated into such groups as the Golden Dawn. Enochian and Kabalistic magicians maintained that the four main Hebrew archangels guarded the four quarters and directions. The directions were also known as Castles. Uriel, or Auriel, represented the Earth Element in the North and had the color black. In Hebrew, the North was called Shemal and considered to be on an individual's left side.

Even tarot cards are related to the four Elements. The meaning of each card of each suit of the Minor Arcana relates in some manner to the Element it represents. In tarot, Earth is symbolized by pentacles, disks, or coins.

The Elements also affect the four levels of the human life and the soul mates who are drawn to us. The Earth Element directly affects the physical or body level. Air Influences the mental attitude. Water affects emotion, as Fire affects motive, intents, and determination

Earth Element Characteristics

Direction: North (South in the Southern Hemisphere).

Description: solid or dense matter; anything having a solid form. In Welsh, *Calas*, which means, "everything hard or firm in structure."

Elemental Spirits: certain types of faeries, elves, gnomes, dwarves, and trolls.

Color: traditionally green. Scottish and Irish: black.

Archangel: Uriel or Auriel.

Ruler of the Element: Ghob, Gob, or Ghom.

Time: midnight and winter.

Plane: physical.

Senses: touch.

Property: cold and dry.

Power Animal of Light: bear, turtle.

Power Animal of Dark: wolf, lynx.

Tattwas: *Prithivi*, a yellow square.

Tarot Suit: pentacles or disks.

Kabalistic World: Assiah, or the Material World.

Symbols: rocks and gemstones, mountains, plains, fields, soil, caves, mines.

Astrological Signs: Taurus, Virgo, Capricorn.

Personality Traits: positive: responsibility, stability, thoroughness, purpose in life, endurance and persistence, respectfulness. Negative: rigidity, stubbornness, vacillation, lack of conscience, unwillingness to change.

Magickal Tools: altar pentacle, stone altar, crystals, stones of any kind.

Ritual Work: wealth, prosperity, treasures, surrendering self-will, empathy, stability, success, business, employment, natural fertility, healing physical illnesses.

The Elemental Spirits of Earth

The major Elemental Spirits of the Earth Element are certain types of faeries, elves, gnomes, dwarves, and trolls. It is important to know how to work with these beings, for they can, and do, affect your environment as well as your physical body. Each of these classes of beings must be approached and worked with in different ways. To attract and work with these spirits, one must know as much as possible about each kind and what they can do with the Earth Element energies. Their traditional king is Gob, Ghom, or Ghob.

Although several types of unfriendly Earth Elementals are listed here, you should know how to work with them or defend yourself against them, if necessary. Most negative-leaning Elementals are not basically evil. Rather, they are part of the positive-negative balance of energy needed to create and control through each Element. It is only when the delicate balance of energies is upset that the destructive, mischievous nature of these beings becomes apparent. During these times, all psychic humans should work to restore the balance of the Elements. This is best done by knowing how to work and interact with all the Elementals.

Bogies

Other names for this wide range of mischievous beings are Bogey-men, Bogles, Boggies, Boggans, Bogey-beasts, and Ballybogs.

Although they live in semi- or complete darkness, these Elementals are not usually harmful to humans. Their preferences for homes are cellars, caves, hollow trees, abandoned mines, deep cupboards, barns, lofts, and under sinks. They especially like places that are cluttered, such as junk shops, tool sheds, secondhand stores, and messy offices. Sometimes, they will take up residence in schools, where they have many opportunities to cause problems.

They have wispy, rather vague bodies with hollow, gleaming eyes. If you happen to surprise a bogey, you will only see a quick flash of movement that disappears instantly from view, and you will feel an unpleasant disturbance in the air. Ordinarily they only come out at night when it is quiet to do minor mischief and frighten humans. They like to hide things, mix up stacks of papers, and hover behind people to make them uneasy and have goose bumps. Causing humans to be fearful of the dark and night is their favorite pastime.

Magickal Uses: You should never invite bogies into your home for any reason. They are too unpredictable to help with spells and too difficult to get rid of once they are established inside your house.

Brownies

When people hear the name "brownies," they immediately make the connection with Scotland, the original land of the European brownie. However, there are similar beings in North Africa called Yumboes, and in China known as Choa Phum Phi. In Wales, brownies are known as Bwbachod; this branch distinctly detests ministers and teetotalers. The clan on the Isle of Manx are called the Fenoderee.

We have only stories of male brownies. However, there must be female ones also, but far too shy to be seen. These Elementals are about 3 feet tall with hairy bodies, rather flat-looking faces, black eyes, slightly pointed ears, and long, dexterous fingers. They derived their name from the brown suits, capes, and hats they wear. On very rare occasions, a brownie will appear in green clothing.

Most brownies attach themselves to families and houses, where they come out at night to be helpful. Some of them stay with a family for generations. Those that haven't chosen a family with which to live inhabit hollow trees and deserted buildings or ruins. Although cheerful and friendly with humans, all brownies do not like ministers or humans who cheat, lie, or make messes.

Old stories say the brownies helped with the farm work. Today, brownies have adapted to modern civilization, but not machinery. They help by tending to house plants, soothing children, or entertaining your pets.

Brownies should not be thanked for their help or given gifts; this will make them leave. However, being friendly with them and leaving out an occasional buttered scone will let them know they are appreciated. It is very good luck to entice a brownie to live in your house, for they repel any invasions by goblins or other small malicious beings.

Magickal Uses: Finding a new residence, friendships, and removing negative Elementals.

Dwarves

The tales of dwarves all come from the Scandinavian and Germanic countries of Northern Europe. The Northern Germans and Scandinavians call the underground dwarf cities the Land of the Nibelungen, or Niebelungen.

Dwarves can be as tall as 3 feet and their heads are large in proportion to the rest of their bodies. Their skin, hair, and eyes are earth colors, and their faces weathered and creased, even as children.

Because of their close connection with the metals and gems of the earth, as well as the Earth Element itself, the dwarves live in vast caves or tunnel systems underground. They do not all live together as one huge clan, but live in smaller groups in various rocky or mountainous areas.

They are experts in forging metal into a variety of forms and polishing gems. Some of their created objects are infused with magickal powers, to help humans, deities, and dwarves. For example, they made Odin's spear and ring, Freyja's powerful necklace and the magickal sow she sometimes rode, and Freyr's boat that could be folded and carried in his pocket.

Dwarves are usually friendly to humans, unless they are harassed or treated rudely. If miners accidentally break into one of their tunnels or seams of ore, and are polite, these small beings will tell the men where to find another vein of the ore they are seeking. However, if any human treats a dwarf with disrespect, they will suffer a long line of bad luck.

These Elemental Spirits use their written language to engrave magickal names and protective powers onto the objects they forge. However, they do not write down their history. Instead, they train bards, much as the Celts did, to remember and recite the entire history of a specific colony of dwarves and all major events that happened in the dwarf kingdoms.

Because dwarves live and work so closely with the vibrations of the earth, they have great powers over gems, stones, and metals. They are particularly proud of their work in cutting and shaping crystals for magickal uses. They consider themselves the guardians of all treasures hidden in the earth.

Magickal Uses: All magickal work with crystals, gems, and stones; the use of metals; making jewelry; and prosperity in general.

Elves

Elves are closely related to faeries. However, there are many differences in their appearance, culture, interaction with nature, and the ways they respond to humans.

Elves are more likely than faeries to have pointed ears and slightly tipped eyes and eyebrows. They are also lighter in skin coloring than faeries, and have striking shades of green and woodland brown eyes.

They live in small groups in forests or groves of trees. If an elf is ever seen away from trees, he or she is on a journey from one place to another. They are so closely tied to the energy of the forests that they cannot exist long outside the energy field of the trees. Human gardens and yards that have trees planted in them often become resting places for traveling elves or sanctuaries for solitary elves.

There appears to be a racial connection between the elves and the Fey, or human-size faeries. They frequently study and work together. Both clans of Elementals practice fighting techniques, as well as studying various other crafts, from blacksmithing to healing. Both have strong feelings toward song, dance, and poetry, as well as very powerful connections to all creatures and flora of nature. Elves are known for their great ability to foretell the future.

As with the Fey, the elves are divided into two classes: the light and the dark elves. The dark elves are much more distrustful of humans and rarely have much to do with them.

Magickal Uses: Writing, music, healing, learning rituals and spellwork, learning the use of herbs and Earth power, public speaking.

Faeries

Faeries are probably the most recognized Elemental Spirits associated with the Earth Element. They are the most frequently seen or felt by humans. Perhaps because they are so closely tied to the planet itself, they live half in/ half out of this plane of existence at all times. However, most people do not realize that there are two distinct classes of faeries: the Small Folk and the fey. To me, this distinction makes faeries one of the most interesting of Elemental Spirits with which we have contact.

When humans speak of faeries, they generally mean the small, humanoid beings seen in nature and flower settings, the ones that appear to have wings. Actually, the wings are emanations of energy that allows these creatures to "fly" from one place to another, one plane of existence to another. In folktales, these Elemental Spirits are called the Little People or Small Folk, to distinguish them from their larger relatives.

The faeries who are intertwined with the Earth Element are those who care for flowers, trees, other wild plants, and specific areas of land. Their areas of influence range from the garden outside your door to the wild, uninhabited places where humans rarely go. This particular type of faery is most likely to interact with humans, sometimes taking up residence with a human family during the cold seasons of the year. There are even certain faeries who make up a subspecies called house faeries. Their primary residence is a human home that is faery-friendly. These homes often have children and/or pets. At other times, these are simply the residences of humans who believe in faeries.

The fey, or human-size faeries, live in groves and deep mountains, seldom near human habitations. However, they do, on occasion, journey to be with a certain chosen human to teach and aid him or her. These are the faeries of folktales who intermarried with humans and had children. The fey are the most intellectually and spiritually advanced of the Faery World.

They are divided into two Courts, neither of which is evil. There is the Seelie Court (a Scottish term), which works only with White Magick. The Unseelie Court works more in the area of Gray Magick. Neither, however, works with Black Magick. Because of centuries of past experience, neither is trusting of humans. It takes much more effort and time to befriend the fey than it does the Small Folk.

The fey also oversee the Small Folk to teach and protect them. The larger faeries realize their relationship to their smaller cousins, and do what they can to help them.

Although the fey build their houses and courts in the deep forests and mountains, their dwellings are on the ground. The houses of the Small Folk can be found nearly everywhere, even in the deserts. They build their little houses under the roots of big trees, in old burrows, in unused birdhouses, and every convenient spot in nature that allows them to be close to the plants for which they are responsible.

Magickal Uses: Gardening, communing with nature, to gain self-confidence and poise, prosperity, good health, to learn ancient secrets, magickal chants, and dance.

Fox Spirits

Also known as fox faeries, these magickal beings originated in Japan and China. Whether they are ancient reddish colored foxes half-transformed or humans possessed by the spirit of a fox, no one knows for certain. Some of them live for centuries, even reincarnating if killed. Stories say that the fox spirit amplifies its magickal powers by the pearl it carries in its mouth or holds under its tail. Any psychic human can identify a fox spirit that appears in human form by the small flame over its head.

To break any spell that is cast on you by one of these beings, you must get it to look into still water. The sight of its reflection will break the spell and illusion, as will hearing a barking dog. However, if the fox spirit is 1,000 years old, these methods will not affect it. Fox spirits that have reached this age are no longer reddish in color, but have white or golden fur, and nine tails. They also rarely bother to play tricks on humans.

Fox spirits are masters of illusion and trickery. If they want to steal something, there is no way the theft can be prevented. Security and distance are no barriers to a fox spirit. Although not entirely negative, these spirits can be a mixed blessing if called upon to aid in spells. The result of the spell must be one that satisfies the fox spirit in some way, or they will change the magickal energy just enough so that you do not get exactly what you wanted.

In Japan, Inari is called the fox goddess and the spirit of the rice. Her main temple is at Kyoto. In the Lydian area of ancient Greece, one form of the god Dionysus was a fox. His priestesses were known as Bassarids; they wore fox skins.

In China, fox spirits were said to cause misfortune and accidents if they were annoyed or upset by humans. The extremely troublesome spirits were exorcised, but little houses were made for the others. By making the fox spirits comfortable and burning incense for them, they had no incentive to be troublesome.

Magickal Uses: Any spell that calls for trickery and/or stealth. These Elementals are tricky to work with, so take great care.

Gnomes

The word "gnome" originated in the Greek language and comes from the words *genomus* (earth dweller) or *gnoma* (the knowing ones). This race of small beings was known throughout northern Europe. In lowland Germany, the gnomes were called *Erdmanleins*, but were known as *Heinzemannchens* in the Alpine areas. Denmark and Norway knew them as *Nisse*, while in Sweden they were called the *Tomtgubbe*. The Balkan countries had several names for gnomes: *Gnom*, *Djude*, and *Mano*.

Although gnomes have a wide variety of forms and types, none of them are taller than 12 inches. Usually, they adopt the physical appearance of the culture in which they live, however, the older males always have a long beard, and the married females wear a headscarf. Gnomes frequently live for several hundred years. They are rarely malicious or dangerous, but, if their habitat is harmed or destroyed, they will retaliate.

Gnomes prefer to make their homes in dimly lit forests or the under the roots of large trees. They will often take over an abandoned burrow and enlarge it to suit their needs. If they live close to sympathetic humans, they will sometimes live in rock gardens, empty birdhouses, or among the roots of thick shrubbery. They live in harmony with all nature, gathering cereals, mushrooms, and root vegetables that they store in underground pantries. They are hard-working, good-natured beings, who care for all the plants and animals in their area.

Although gnomes may appear physically similar to the culture in which they live, their clothing varies little from area to area. The males wear a tunic, tight leg coverings, multi-colored stockings, pointed-toed shoes, and a red conical hat. The females wear blouses, long skirts, aprons, multi-colored stockings, pointed-toed shoes, and headscarves, if they are married.

Gnomes do not like technology. They prefer to do their weaving and woodcarving by hand. They also act as healers for the animals in their area.

Because of their close ties with the Earth Element, gnomes can raise magickal energy by dancing, can predict the future, are great natural healers, and have the ability to influence changes in animate and inanimate objects. They know the age-old secrets of using energy patterns.

Magickal Uses: Healing, changes, raising magickal energy, understanding universal energy patterns and how to use them, and divination.

Goblins

No one is certain where goblins originated, just that they spread across France to Britain from the Pyrenees Mountains. Annoying, troublesome beings, they were known as *Gobelins* in Germany, *Brags* in Scotland, and *Robin Goblins* or *Hobgoblins* in Britain. In parts of Scotland, this being is called a *Boggart* and in northern England a *Padfoot*.

Although goblins have a human-like form, other Earth Elementals will not allow them in their company because of the goblins' tendency for evil mischief and cunning. Goblins do not even get along with other negative Elementals.

Some goblins have learned how to alter their size from very small to almost human size. Usually, humans see them only as a dark blob that gives off malicious energy. If they materialize in their true form, they are hairy, have wide evil grins, and mean faces. They come in all shades of brown, with stubby ears and glittering eyes.

Goblins are strongest and most active at night, when they weave nightmares or fill the house with bad luck. They can easily communicate with such insects as hornets, mosquitoes, flies, and wasps. They then send hordes of these insects to attack humans and other warm blooded animals.

If they are exorcised from a house, goblins will wander around in gangs, taking temporary shelter in clefts in rocks or twisting roots of old trees. Their victims then are any lonely traveler on the road.

Magickal Uses: Not recommended at all! Once goblins, like bogies, get inside a house, they are extremely difficult to get rid of. They are such a nuisance that magicians will not allow them around.

Gremlins

Gremlins are Earth Elementals that are distantly related to goblins and gnomes. They resemble goblins and love to do mischief and harm to tools and machinery. They are experts at fouling up any piece of equipment from airplanes to computers. Many people think gremlins only came into being during World War II when they were said to cause airplane problems. However, gremlins have been around since humans invented tools beyond a rock and a stick. Their greatest joy is to make human lives as miserable as possible. Traditionally, it is said that every house and business has at least one gremlin in residence.

Magickal Uses: Working with gremlins is not recommended at all!

Kobolds

Kobolds have a mixed reputation that I believe comes from the way they are treated by humans. If they are mistreated, insulted, or ignored, they will throw things and cause all manner of inconvenience in a house. In Germany and Finland, kobolds were known only as mischievous beings. Some churches in Finland kept exorcists who specialized in evicting kobolds from houses.

However, if treated with respect and provided with a little food and shelter, the ordinary kobold can be very helpful. They can create a pleasant atmosphere, good luck, and a healthy garden. Although rarely seen by humans, kobolds are described as little old men with wrinkled faces. They wear brown knee pants, red felt hats, and smoke pipes. No females have ever been seen.

Magickal Uses: (Be certain you treat all kobolds with respect, and only call upon those who are friendly toward you.) Good luck; help in making a project, event, or relationship run smoothly.

Old Lady of the Elder

Many cultures believe that elder trees have special magickal powers and are protected by a strange Earth Elemental known as the old lady of the elder. People in Scandinavian countries called this being the *Hyldermoder* (Elder Mother). Today, in parts of Germany and Denmark, the country people tip their hats when they pass an elder tree.

Although rarely seen by humans, the best times to look for the old lady of the elder is in the spring when the elder trees bear their white blossoms, or in autumn when the black elder berries ripen. This Elemental likes to be out at night when the moon is full. She appears as an elderly lady with a elder bark-colored gown, black apron, and white cap and shawl. With this coloring, she is almost invisible when she moves through the tree shadows. She always carries a staff cut from an elder branch.

This Elemental supplies the elder tree with magickal powers, which can be tapped by humans for either White or Black Magick. The flowers, berries, and bark can be used to make salves and potions. Before cutting any elder wood, it is best to ask permission and pour an offering of milk and honey onto the ground under the tree. Then the branches can be used to make wands or rune sticks. It is not considered lucky to use the wood for mundane purposes.

Magickal Uses: Divination, especially the runes; gaining herb wisdom; and learning how to properly use a wand.

Pixies

In Cornwall, England, and the area around it, these small Elemental beings are called Piskies. From their name comes the word *pesky*. This word very aptly describes their temperament and behavior. No one knows where pixies originated, but there has always been animosity between them and the faeries. Often this erupts into battles.

Although about the size of a human hand, pixies have the power and ability to increase or decrease in size. Some of the males can even take on a full-grown human appearance. Pixies have bright red hair, green eyes, an upturned nose, and pointed ears. They wear green outfits that let them blend into the fields and forests, to become almost invisible. They love flower gardens and herb beds, with foxglove and mushrooms being their favorite plants. Often, they will wear a mushroom or foxglove blossom as a hat.

Pixies and other Elementals are most active and likely to be seen at Beltane (May) and Summer Solstice (June). At these times, the Elementals of each Element have their fairs, gatherings, and parties where they dance, sing, and make merry.

Pixies will not directly harm humans. However, they like to play tricks, such as lead hikers and travelers astray until they are lost. The old term of *pixie-led* refers to a human who becomes so confused by the pixie tricks that she or he wanders aimlessly about and has trouble remembering things.

To keep on the good side of pixies, if they happen to live in your area, leave out a bowl of water for washing their babies and sweep clean a place for dancing.

Magickal Uses: These Elementals are not reliable to work with.

Trolls

These unusual Elementals are called *Trolds* in Sweden and *Hill Men* or *Berg People* in Denmark. They originated in the Scandinavian areas and then spread around the world. In Iceland, these beings, known as the *Illes*, live underground and come out only at night. The people of the Feroes Islands call them the *Foddenskkmaend* (Underground People).

Trolls come in all shapes and sizes. Often indistinct in form, and becoming invisible at will, they have deep, rumbling voices, are extremely strong, and are not too intelligent. Their skin is like lichen-covered stone, and they have almost no neck. Some of them, however, are experts at mechanics, construction, and working at a forge.

These Elementals prefer to live in the mountains, moorlands, deep forests, or underground in dark enclosed places.

Even the smallest hill often contains a troll home. However, some trolls have adapted to human cities by residing in abandoned concrete or brick buildings. They can also be found in underpasses and storm drains.

Trolls do not venture out into sunlight during the day, as this light is incompatible with their cellular structure and causes them to become immobile. They prefer to walk about at night or at dusk. Some of the younger ones run in gangs and behave like bullies, especially toward humans. To trolls, humans are very ugly and do not smell good.

Magickal Uses: It is best to let a troll helper appear without calling them. Never command them, or they will be troublesome. These Elementals are great protectors. They can also help you learn the secrets of stones, how to work with metal, the importance of music and dance in rituals, and the science of mechanics.

Earth Element Meditation

Learning to meditate is very valuable, both for gaining information and for learning the concentration needed to perform working magick. The same type of visualization is used during spellwork as in meditation. You must be able, in your mind, to see each astral movement and step you make and the end result when you are finished.

Meditation is also quieting and healing to the body, mind, and spirit. Whenever you do any of the meditations explained in this book, first prepare with the following methods. Every meditation will begin and end in the same way. You will never be in any danger during a meditation as you are free to awake at any time.

> *Sit in a comfortable chair with your hands in your lap and your feet flat on the floor. Make certain you will not disturbed by the telephone, someone at the door, pets, or any other people in the house. It may be helpful to play a CD of soft nature sounds, to mask any slight background noises. If you put each meditation on a tape, leave spaces in the appropriate places so that you have time to explore or listen to whoever is speaking to you.*
>
> *Visualize a brilliant white light surrounding and penetrating your body. This is your protection throughout the meditation. Now, slowly begin to relax your body, beginning at the feet and ending at the head. During this time, breathe steadily and evenly. Breathe out all the negatives and troubles in your life. Breathe in the white light of healing and balance.*

Experiencing the Earth

> *See yourself standing in an open space with tall ancient stones surrounding the area in a circle. It is night, and a full moon shines gently down upon you. The velvety night sky is so clear you can see every star. The grass under your bare feet is short and soft.*

As you look around, you begin to feel a pleasant tingling on the soles of your feet. You notice a shimmering faint distortion of the air for several feet above the ground. You realize that this is the earth's energy. You kneel and press both hands against the ground. Now, you feel the tingling on the palms of your hands and your lower legs.

This energy is so relaxing and inviting that you lie down on the ground with your arms and legs spread out. In this manner, every part of your body is exposed to the rising energy of the earth. You lie there, soaking up the energy and looking at the bright stars overhead.

Suddenly, you realize that your body is very slowly sinking into the ground. You are not afraid or harmed in any way by this experience. You have no difficulty breathing or moving. You relax even more as the earth's energy totally surrounds you.

You feel this strong, healing energy penetrating every bone and organ of your body. Your body soaks up the healing like a dry sponge. Your bones seem stronger. Any physical problems you have are now being slowly healed. You notice a greater feeling of strength in your bones and blood. Your heart and lungs are working better. Your thought processes are clearer. Your feelings and thoughts about your life are more centered and balanced.

You begin to experience the earth with all your senses. Your skin is ultra-sensitive to the texture of the soil and small stones. You experience the feel of these in a totally new way. You notice the difference in smell between the soil itself and various stones that are in the ground near you. You move one arm slowly through the ground. As your fingers touch the soil and the stones, you smell their unique scents and are surprised at the differences you experience. You relax once more and, at once, hear the vibrational heartbeat of the earth. It is a comforting sound. You find your own vibrations automatically readjusting to match those of the earth.

Slowly, you rise up out of the ground and stretch your arms toward the black sky. Then you kneel and gently pat the earth with both hands in thanks for the energy you were given. You walk around the circle of stones, touching each one as you go by. You can feel the earth's energies vibrating through the stones, mingling with the stones' own energy and becoming stronger before that power is sent out around the world.

You take a deep breath of the cool, pleasant night air before you step outside the circle of old moss-dotted stones.

*You think of your physical body. You slide
down the tunnel of light into that body. You open
your eyes. The meditation is finished.*

Earth Elemental Meditation

This meditation is to let you experience the presence
of certain Earth Elementals in a safe, protected environment. Later, you can visit different Elementals, using the
same meditation.

*Sit in a comfortable chair with your hands in
your lap and your feet flat on the floor. Make certain you will not be disturbed by the telephone,
someone at the door, pets, or any other people in
the house. It may be helpful to play a CD of soft
nature sounds, to mask any slight background
noises. If you put each meditation on a tape, leave
spaces in the appropriate places so that you have
time to explore or listen to whoever is speaking
to you.*

*Visualize a brilliant white light surrounding
and penetrating your body. This is your protection throughout the meditation. Now, slowly begin
to relax your body, beginning at the feet and ending
at the head. During this time, breathe steadily and*

evenly. Breathe out all the negatives and troubles in your life. Breathe in the white light of healing and balance.

See yourself standing in a beautiful meadow with trees all around. Here and there, across the meadow, you see bright patches of color mixed in with the tall green grass. A light scent of flowers carries on the faint breeze that touches your face. The blue sky overhead is broken by clumps of fluffy white clouds. Deep, cool shadows lie under the trees at the edges of the meadow.

The bright flowers that dot the meadow are each surrounded by small hovering creatures. At first you think these are butterflies, but when you look closer, you see they are the Small Folk, the tiny faeries. Several of the faeries come closer to you, and one of them settles on your hand. They welcome you to their world and tell you about their activities among the plants and flowers of this meadow.

Within a few minutes, you see two tall figures step out of the shadowed forest and walk toward you. As they get closer, the tall man with the bow slung across his shoulder pushes his hair back from his face. You see his slightly pointed ears and the tipped eyes, and know he is an elf. He has a specially forged elf-sword hanging from his belt. His mottled dark and light green tunic and trousers would make him nearly invisible in the any forest. The woman with him is dressed in a green gown and holds a crystal-tipped wand in one hand. You recognize her as one of the fey, the larger faeries.

"Welcome to our world," the woman says, as she smiles at you. "We have come to introduce you to many of the Earth Elementals. We will be your guides and protectors during this important journey."

The elf points out across the meadow, and you see a path open through the grass. The path leads to the thick forest that surrounds this open place. He gives you a warm smile as he leads the way down the path. The fey woman walks beside you to talk as the two of you follow the elf.

"Do not be frightened at any time," the woman says. "Some of the Earth Elementals we meet will not be reliable, but they cannot harm us."

"Between Gwendell's magick and mine, they would not dare," the elf says as he glances at you over his shoulder.

Suddenly, a group of small red-haired beings leap out of the tall grass beside the path. They are dressed in green clothing and each wears a foxglove blossom as a hat.

"Pixies! What pranks do you plan today, Little Ones?" The fey woman frowns at the prancing figures, but they stay well out of reach.

"Pixie-led," one of the small beings calls out.

"You know that does not work on elves or faeries," the elf warrior answers and keeps walking along the path.

"We have no time for play," the fey woman says. "Go home."

The pixies run off into the grass. However, a sudden shower of dried leaves and small twigs pelts the three of you. The cackle of pixie laughter follows you as the elf leads the way under the first trees of the forest.

As the forest gets thicker the farther in you go, you begin to grow uneasy. The shadows are thick and heavy under the dense foliage, cutting off all but a few stray beams of sunlight. Goose bumps rise on your arms just seconds before you feel a puff of air on the back of your neck and hear a wicked laugh close to your ear.

"Goblins!" The elf warrior draws his magickal sword and quickly outlines a circle in the earth around the three of you.

"*Come out, come out. Come out to play with us.*" *A chorus of malicious voices comes from behind the trees on each side of the path.*

You stare into the thick shadows until you see a number of strange faces. The creatures have stubby ears, wide grins, and glittering eyes. They send out waves of fear that make you move closer to the elf warrior and Fey woman.

"*They cannot harm us,*" *the woman says, as she raises her magick wand.* "*Show yourselves,*" *she orders.* "*By the power of Earth, Air, Fire, and Water, I command you.*"

Reluctantly, the goblins slowly come out of their hiding places in the shadows. They stay well clear of the circle drawn by the sword. Their bodies are abnormally thin and long, with wide heads and wispy strands of hair.

"*You are no fun,*" *one of them says.*

"*You know the power I command?*" *the woman asks, and the goblins all nod.* "*Then be gone! Trouble us no more. It is forbidden for you to frighten travelers using this path.*"

The goblins quickly disappear into the forest, grumbling as they go. Within seconds, they are out of sight, and the feeling of maliciousness disappears from the atmosphere.

The elf slides his sword back into the sheath as he walks on up the path. Before very long, the

*trail comes out onto a rocky hillside. About half
way up the hill you see the dark opening of a cave.
Your companions urge you up the path to the cave
entrance.*

*"Hello," the elf calls out, as he stands at the
cave opening. "May we enter?"*

*"Yes, come in," a gravelly voice says. "The
sun is not down yet, but I am awake."*

*The three of you go into the dark cave. There
is a spark near the back of the cave, and a lan-
tern shines in the darkness. You see a very large
boulder covered with moss lying against the cave
wall. While you watch in fascination, this boulder begins to take on a more human shape. Two
eyes open in the stones. A mouth yawns. Then the
troll stretches and stands up, and you see this
Elemental in its true form.*

*"We have brought a human to meet you," the
faery women say. "This one is on the path of learning about the Elements and the Elementals."*

*"Welcome then," the troll says, and holds out
a massive hand for you to shake. It feels like warm
stone against your skin. "It is wise of you to learn
about us, for you and the entire universe are made
from mixtures of the Elements."*

*You now ask any questions about the Earth
Element you wish of the troll, the elf, and the faery*

woman. They also talk about some of the Earth Elementals that you haven't met on this journey.

"You must return to your time and place," the elf finally says, as he leads you to the cave opening. "Think upon what you have seen and learned."

"Goodbye," the faery woman says and smiles as she waves her wand at you.

You think of your physical body. You slide down the tunnel of light into that body. You open your eyes. The meditation is finished.

Magickal Uses of Earth Energy

Always consider all the outcomes of a spell before doing magick. You do not want to harm yourself or others. It is best to defend against or bind troublesome people, even return their negative energy to them, rather than become involved in a war of magickal spells.

I have one main rule for performing magick: "Face it. Trace it. Erase it." In other words, face the problem. Is the problem real or imaginary? Did you create it? Is it the creation of someone else? If you caused your problem, undo any mistakes you made and work for harmony and balance. If the problem is not of your creation or appears to be imaginary (you can find no logical sense in its happening), trace the trouble to its source. This step may require doing meditations or using divinatory aids. Also use common sense. Sometimes negative energy is left behind or sent by thoughts of a person and is not a deliberate spell on you. All this helps you to determine if you need to do a spell at all, or what kind of spell would be most useful. "Erase it" means just what it says: Get rid of the problem. Do this in the easiest and safest manner possible. Calling upon the Elementals for help is a good, natural means of defense and protection.

Those who practice magick soon learn that there are periods when the manifestations just don't seem to arrive in a timely manner, regardless of what we do or how we do it. We begin to get discouraged and fall into negative thinking patterns, thus negating all our efforts. Instead of becoming discouraged, we need to learn to hang in there just a bit longer. Manifestation as the result of magickal spells is rather like the explanation in quantum physics of reaching critical mass. An electron will only reach critical mass and change when 51 percent of it is vibrating at a higher frequency. When 51 percent is reached, it automatically pulls the remaining 49 percent up into the higher vibration. Therefore, if we continue to empower the magick until its vibration and our internal visualization reach 51 percent, absolutely nothing can stop the manifestation of our desire. It can be very difficult to judge when the 51 percent mark is reached. That is why most spells are repeated three, five, seven, or nine times (a figure usually determined by the magician). Each concentrated repetition adds energy to the spell, causing it to vibrate at a higher rate each time. By building and strengthening the spell's energy, and keeping our thinking positive, we can reach the critical mass of 51 percent and manifest our desires in the physical world.

Earth Spells

Whenever anyone does spell work, the person should carefully think through all possible repercussions and possible results. The spell worker is responsible for anyone she or he creates. The types of spell also should be carefully chosen and the correct mental intent requires putting the work into it. Never use spells to control another person. This infringes upon their free will and will rebound on the spell worker, causing all kinds of negative results.

Gift to the Faeries

If you want to give a special gift to the faeries, elves, and other friendly Earth Elementals, mix a little honey in a small amount of milk. Take this outside to your yard, or another place in nature, and pour it over a rock. Then tell the Elementals how you appreciate their existence and help. Just use your own words. You can also sprinkle a pinch of ground ginger on the rock as an additional offering. If you don't have an appropriate rock in your yard or flowerbeds, either find one in nature or buy one. Flat rocks are excellent for this purpose, but any rock will do.

Candle Magick Spells

I have tried to keep suggested magickal supplies to the kind that can be found easily and cheaply. Incense can be bought in stick or cone form. Many of the herbs can be found in the kitchen cupboard, or are easily obtained at a local health food store or New Age shop. Buy the herbs ground, if possible. If you have to get them in their whole form, grind them into a powder yourself, using a mortar and pestle or a small coffee bean grinder that you save for only magickal work. Most oils are available in New Age shops, health food stores, grocery outlets, or cooking stores. For a lists of all correspondences, see the Appendix.

I prefer to use votive candles whenever possible. You can buy them nearly anywhere. Just hold onto the wick and remove the metal tab on the bottom before using them. The metal tab can get quite hot and crack a glass votive holder. To avoid this problem, and to provide a safe place to allow a candle to burn out, I use a small cast iron cauldron. By coating the inside bottom of the cauldron with oil, you can easily remove the candle wax when the spell is finished.

To bring things into your life, you rub oil onto a candle from the wick to the bottom. To take things out of your life, you rub the oil on the candle from the bottom to the wick.

The stones required can be small tumbled pieces found in New Age shops or your local rock shop.

It is best to keep your magickal supplies to the simple and easily found. Then you can relax when you do a ritual, instead of worrying about the cost of the materials.

Remember, you will only use very small amounts of herbs and oils in any spellwork. You can use either a nail or a small knife to carve words or designs onto the side of the candle.

Prosperity

- ✧ a green candle
- ✧ honeysuckle incense
- ✧ cinnamon oil
- ✧ ground cloves
- ✧ one or more yellow stones
- ✧ one or more green stones
- ✧ a safe candle holder
- ✧ a nail or something sharp to cut a design into the candle
- ✧ Paper towels for rolling the candle in the ground herbs, and for wiping oil from your hands

Timing: best done during a waxing moon up to, and including, the full moon.

Spell: Have all your materials in the place where you will allow the candle to burn completely out. If it is possible, you should have a small space or table that you use as a magickal altar. Lay out a paper towel and lightly spread a small amount of ground cloves onto the towel. The candle does not need to be completely or thickly coated.

Begin by lighting the incense and placing it into its holder.

Scratch or incise a dollar sign into the side of the candle. Put a small amount of cinnamon oil into the palm of your power hand (the hand you write with). Rub the candle from the wick to the bottom with this oil as you chant:

> *Wealth, success, prosperity,*
> *All of these now come to me.*

Roll the candle lightly over the powdered cloves until the oil has picked up as much as possible. Set the candle into its holder. Wipe the oil and herbs from your hands with the clean paper towel. Place the green and yellow stones near the candle. If you have enough stones, form them into a ring around the candle and its holder.

Light the candle. Chant:

> *Earth Elementals, wild and free,*
> *Send your mighty powers to me.*
> *Let them join with my own,*
> *To create a prosperous form.*

Concentrate on your desire to be prosperous for at least five minutes while you watch the candle flame. At the end of five minutes, repeat the chant.

Leave the candle to burn completely out. When the wax is cold, remove it from the holder and dispose of it.

Finding a Job

✧ a brown candle
✧ a magenta candle
✧ a zodiac color candle to represent you
✧ frankincense incense
✧ powdered dragon's blood
✧ peppermint oil

✧   brown and orange stones
✧   three safe candle holders
✧   a nail or something sharp to cut a
     design into the candle
✧   Paper towels for rolling the candle
     in the ground herbs, and for wiping
     oil from your hands.

Timing: best done during a waxing moon up to, and including, the full moon.

Spell: Set the three candle holders in a triangular pattern on your altar. Place the stones near the holders. Spread out a paper towel and sprinkle a small amount of powdered dragon's blood resin onto the towel. Light the frankincense incense.

Scratch a simplified arrow (a straight line with a V at the end of it) pointing to a big X onto the side of each candle, using a nail or a small knife. The arrow may be scratched so that it goes around the candle or points toward the top, or wick end. The X represents protection, while the arrow symbolizes swift forward movement of your spell's power.

Put a small amount of peppermint oil in the palm of your power hand. Rub this onto each candle, from the wick to the bottom. Then roll each candle in the powdered dragon's blood and put it into a holder. Do this with one candle at a time. As you rub the oil onto each candle, chant:

Faster than an arrow's flight,
My desire is fulfilled this night.

Light the zodiac candle that represents you, and say:

> *I will do everything I can to seek a job.*

Light the brown candle, and say:

> *Earth Elementals, all those who know the*
> *joy of creating, I ask for your help.*

Light the magenta candle, and say:

> *Faster than a lightning bolt,*
> *this spell manifests my desire.*

Hold your hands so that the palms face the burning candles. Chant:

> *This spell's power goes far and wide,*
> *To bring opportunities to my side.*
> *The perfect job appears for me.*
> *This is my will. So shall it be.*

Concentrate on your desire to find the perfect job for you for at least five minutes while you watch the candle flame. At the end of five minutes, repeat the chant.

Leave the candles to burn completely out. When the wax is cold, remove it from the holders and dispose of it.

Protection

- ✧ a black candle
- ✧ patchouli incense
- ✧ frankincense oil
- ✧ black stones

- ✧ one white stone
- ✧ basil
- ✧ a safe candle holder
- ✧ a nail or something sharp to cut a design into the candle
- ✧ Paper towels for rolling the candle in the ground herbs, and for wiping oil from your hands.

Timing: best done during a waning moon up to, and including, a new moon.

Spell: Begin by lighting the incense and placing it in its holder. Put the one white stone directly between you and the candle. Arrange the black stones on each side. Put the ground basil on a paper towel to one side.

Scratch three large Xs into the side of the candle. Put a few drops of frankincense oil into the palm of your power hand (the hand you write with). Rub the candle from the bottom to the wick with this oil as you chant:

The power of the Earth Element
protects me from all dangers.

Roll the candle in the powdered basil, and place it in the holder. Light the candle and chant:

All negative things go far away,
Leaving only light to stay.
Strong protection surrounds me.
And as I say, so shall it be.

Concentrate on your desire to be protected for at least five minutes while you watch the candle flame. At the end of five minutes, repeat the chant.

Leave the candle to burn completely out. When the wax is cold, remove it from the holder and dispose of it.

Stone Elixirs for Earth Elementals

Stone elixirs have been used in magickal workings for centuries. Like many other things about magick, we have no idea how old the practices and ideas are. Once made, the elixirs will last up to a year. To be certain of the time length, many magicians start the elixirs on a Solstice or an Equinox.

Elixirs can be used on the Third Eye to help find and learn certain knowledge you need. The Third Eye is the spot on the center of your forehead, just above the area between your eyebrows. You can anoint this same spot on another person for healing, protection, or to help them absorb the energy from any spell you do for them. The elixir must match the purpose of the spell, in this case.

A drop of an elixir can also be used as a "thank you" to Elemental Spirits when you are in or near physical representations of their Element. To do this, touch the earth, swish your finger in water, hold the finger up into the wind, or wave your finger over a candle flame. You can use a finger moistened with elixir to touch your door and the area around it to attract or repel certain energies. This is also useful to do with your vehicle.

To make stone elixirs, you will need:

✦ several clean, small (at least two ounce size or bigger) glass bottles with caps

✦ purified or spring water

✦ a small amount of sea salt

✦ a wide-topped glass jar with a lid

✦ the specific stone for the elixir

It is better to have dark colored glass bottles for storing elixirs. However, this isn't always possible, so clear glass bottles, stored in a dark place, are quite acceptable. Never leave your elixirs just sitting around, but put them in a specific, private place.

Make certain all your equipment is clean and dry before you begin the elixirs. Pour at least two ounces of the water into the wide-top glass jar. Drop the stone you plan to use into the water. Tighten the lid on the jar and set it where the sun will shine on it for most of the day. Leave the jar in this position for seven days. At the end of that time, remove the stone from the water. Add a pinch of sea salt, and stir to dissolve. Pour the elixir into the smaller bottles. Label each bottle with the name of the stone used. The stone may be reused after it has "rested" for at least three months.

When you have the wide-topped jar filled with the water and stone, and before you set it in the sunlight, hold the jar in both hands and say the chant appropriate to the stone being used. Some of these chants follow, while others are given in the appropriate chapters on the other Elements.

Obsidian

This stone is useful for protection and removing negative vibrations.

> *Black as the night, you come from the earth,*
> *Where you were formed and given birth.*
> *You absorb all negativity,*
> *To remove all harm and protect me.*

Aventurine

This green stone will attract faeries and elves, as well as prosperity.

> *Good nature spirits, large and small,*
> *Please join me here, as I call*
> *Upon your friendship and prosperity.*
> *This is my will. So mote it be.*

Carnelian

Widely used by the ancient Egyptians, this stone helps with changing your luck and getting control of your life or a situation in your life.

> *Bright color of fast energy,*
> *Change my luck and set me free.*
> *Opportunities to change my path,*
> *Control of my life is all I ask.*

Amethyst

Purple in color, this popular stone can break bad luck or hexes, or help to develop the psychic senses.

Stone of wisdom and power old,
Break me free of bad luck's hold.
Teach to me psychic senses' power,
So I am aware in every hour,
Of vibrations that are not good for me.
This power I claim. So shall it be.

Leopard Agate

This spotted stone can create sudden changes and increase the mental powers.

Leopard-quick, with changing power,
Increase my mental powers to bold
And sharp. Within this magick hour,
Prepare me for the change to hold.

Powering Amulets and Talismans

Most people—even those within the magickal community—think of an amulet and a talisman as being the same thing, or very close to being the same. However, they are not. An *amulet* is a charm, a symbol to protect the wearer against evil. This can be a rabbit's foot, a four-leaf clover, a small horseshoe, the Mediterranean blue bead or blue eye-stone, or other similar things found in nature. A *talisman* is an object produced particularly for a specific individual—a sign or object made to do a special task.

These can be sigils (specifically drawn designs), medicine bags, clear crystal points hung on chains, or little spell bags containing various items. A talisman can also be a metal charm that represents an Elemental Spirit or a specific goal you have in mind. This includes any object that symbolizes a particular Elemental Spirit to you. For example, a plain, ordinary stone can represent trolls, while crystals can symbolize faeries and elves, and an acorn could be for gnomes.

When a talisman is used for an Elemental Spirit, you need to chant the energy of that Spirit into it's symbol. By carrying something with you that reminds you of a particular type of Elemental Spirit, you will have closer communication with that Spirit, as well as learn faster about the Elemental's powers.

A talisman can also be worn or carried to represent the Power Animal with which you might be working. Working with both a Power Animal and an Elemental Spirit from the same Element can aid you greatly in whatever magickal work you are doing. Remember, the dark does not mean evil. It is an energy that balances light. Sometimes, situations or people gather too much light to themselves, just as other times they gather too much dark. The Power Animals can help you to rebalance the problem.

An amulet or a talisman can be fully charged by leaving it lying on a clear crystal or amethyst crystal cluster overnight on the full moon. Crystal clusters work exceptionally well for cleaning and charging other stones, whatever the kind. They also can do the same thing to pieces of jewelry.

The vibrations of the cluster will remove all negative or foreign influences, replacing that with positive vibrations.

Communication With Faeries and Elves

If you plan to make a talisman bag to communicate better with faeries and elves, you will first need a small leather or cloth bag to hold a little metal faery charm and a crystal point. If you choose to use a cloth bag, you might consider getting it in a brown or green color. Then you need to choose appropriate herbs, other stones, and oils to include. You can put a drop or two of the oil on a cotton ball so that it will not soak through.

During a waxing moon, or on a full moon, hold the filled bag in your power hand and chant:

> *Good faeries and elves, so wild and free,*
> *Come, teach your ancient ways to me.*
> *By spark of star and ray of sun,*
> *Our time together has begun.*
> *Element of Earth, now reveal to me,*
> *Your Spirits that I need to see.*
> *Bring closer every nature sprite,*
> *That I can learn from them each night.*

Leave the Elemental bag on a crystal cluster overnight. Then it is charged so that you can carry it with you or leave it on your altar to hold during meditations. You can recharge it every full moon by repeating the chant and putting it on the crystal cluster.

Eventually, you will be drawn to learn how to handle the powers of the dark and light Power Animals of each Element. These animals can be used on the astral plane as guides, and are of value in carrying messages to and from the Elemental Spirits to which they are attached. You can also learn to temporarily assume the magickal energies of these Power Animals when you need to face and resolve a situation that falls under their Element's control.

Working With Power Animals

If you chose to work with a Power Animal, and want to have a physical representation of it to remind yourself of its energies, you can do this in the form of statues, charms, even T-shirts.

The following are examples of chants to call upon and work with the turtle and the wolf, both Power Animals of the Element of Earth, and both closely connected with the nature spirits, especially the fey and elves.

The Turtle

Think about the turtle and its association with the Earth Element. It moves very close to the surface of the ground, thus being in direct contact with the Earth energies. It is slow and exact in its movements, as well as retreating into its shell at any sign of danger. Meditate upon all the other qualities and traits of this Animal of Light. Whenever you decide to work with the turtle, hold its representation in your hands and say:

Earth animal of light,
I ask that you aid me in contacting
the Earth Elemental Spirits.
Help me feel the Earth energies
that surround me.
Open communication for me
with the Elemental Spirits I seek.
I thank you, little turtle.

The Wolf

The association of the wolf with the Earth Element is completely different than that of the turtle. The wolf depends upon tracking, cunning, strength, and swiftness to win its battles and move through life. This type of energy balances that of slowness and patient exactness. Meditate upon all the qualities of this Power Animal of dark. If you decide to work with the wolf, hold a representation of it in both hands and say:

Earth animal of dark,
I seek your help. I need to find the proper places
to meet with the Earth Elemental Spirits.
I need your swift, cunning skills to communicate with,
and learn from these Spirits, so that I can keep this
Element balanced
in my life and in my surroundings.
Thank you, great wolf."

Whenever you have need of the energies expressed by the turtle or wolf, all you need to do is think of them, or touch the symbol that represents them. You will feel their power flow into your body and mind. They will be of great help in contacting and making friends with the Elemental Spirits.

Soul Mate Spell, Part 1

Everyone is concerned with finding his or her soul mate in life. The following spell should only be done if you are single. If you are in a relationship of whatever kind, you need to resolve any problems you have before doing this spell. Resolving the problems will require you to look truthfully at your contribution to the troubled relationship. If you don't see your part, you are doomed to repeat the same mistakes in every relationship you have.

Finding your soul mate does not mean you will never have disagreements or periods of trouble in your relationship. No one is perfect. The difference between a soul mate relationship and any other kind is that soul mates will try harder to communicate, work at solving any disagreements, and be willing to compromise, without either one having control of the other.

The supplies needed for this spell are very simple:

✧   red construction paper
✧   a green pen and crayons

Timing: It is best done on a Friday during a waxing moon. You will find the construction paper and crayons so useful for quick, effective spells, similar to this one, that you should probably purchase a thick pad of paper in various colors and a large box of crayons that will give you a wide selection of hues with which to work. The paper does not need to be larger than nine inches by twelve inches.

This spell will not be completed at this time. You will add to it after you study each of the other Elements and Elemental Spirits. Please give much thought to what you actually seek in a soul mate. Take care that you do not dwell merely on a pleasurable physical image. Every person has more than one soul available, a few of which you will need in order to work out karmic problems. Finding a soul mate does not necessarily mean the two of you will stay together forever if the only connection is the working out of specific past-life troubles.

Spell: Using a green crayon, draw a large heart in the center of one sheet of red construction paper. Write your name above the heart with a pink crayon. With the same crayon, decorate the area around the big heart with many smaller hearts. Think of love and companionship while you are doing this. You may draw other love symbols on the remaining edges of the paper with other colors if you wish.

Now consider all the Earth Element, or physical, qualities you hope to find in a soul mate. This may be as simple as a certain culture, or someone of a specific height. Some people do not like light colored hair. If this is your case, by all means decide on dark hair as a feature you desire. Write all these desired traits inside the large heart with the green pen. And be certain to write "single"! You do not want to be attracted to a person who is married to someone else. Also, specify which gender you want to attract. Do not write too many physical traits. Not only will you need space to include other traits from other Elements at a later time, but if you are far too exact, you limit yourself in your search for your soul mate. In fact, you might exclude the perfect partner by too much exactness.

When you are finished writing, fold both outside edges to the middle of the heart, thus making two little "doors" that hide the heart from view. Hold the folded paper against your chest in the area of your own heart and chant:

> *I call into both time and space,*
> *To find a soul mate is my desire.*
> *I wish my life to be complete*
> *With companionship and loving fire.*
> *My call goes out to all who hear,*
> *To bring to me a soul mate dear.*

If possible, leave this paper on your altar. If there is a possibility someone else might handle the paper, put it away in a safe place. You will need to add more traits to this "soul mate heart" when you finish reading the next chapter on the Element of Air.

THE ELEMENT OF AIR

Like Air, let your mind and ideas fly free.

The Element of Air consists of gaseous, vaporous matter, or anything with an invisible gaseous form. In Welsh, *breath*, means every wind, breeze, respiration, and air. Humans move through air constantly and depend upon it to live. However, we are only aware of air if we are touched by the wind or feel the breath or passing by of someone or something. In the Otherworld, the Element of Air exists in the nebulous form of thoughts and ideas.

This is the idea or concept phase of magick. To have a manifestation be exactly as one wants, the magician must have thought through every angle of the spell—how it will look, how it will act (positive or negative), how it will influence any humans involved in its presence, and if it will be permanent or temporary. Every magician is responsible for every manifestation she or he creates.

The Element of Air plays an important part in human personalities, for it governs the mental processes and the mental body. This body is one of four that each human possesses: physical, mental, emotional, and spiritual. Human thoughts and ideas are very delicate things, easily upset and thrown out of balance by events, relationships, or new information. The Element of Air is one of the Elements likely to be in and out of balance in humans at any given moment. Even the product of the Element itself, in the form of storms and hot desert winds that continue for weeks, can cause imbalances in humans and the way they act and react. For some humans, it is a difficult process to be aware of, control, and/or moderate their thoughts. Illusions may seem to be reality.

The Elemental Spirits of Air are powerful, mysterious, wispy beings of constantly changing form. Unless the magician is very disciplined and trained, these Elementals can be difficult to work with. They are not likely to cause harm if they escape control, but will simply vanish instantly. They are most often experienced in breezes and storms. The Elemental Air Spirits retain an unlimited amount of inspiration, new ideas, and knowledge.

Traditionally, the Elemental Spirits of Air are the *sylphs* and *zephyrs*. However, there are several other creatures representative of the Element of Air, such as one kind of faery found in high mountainous regions, Arabian genies (or the Djinn), gargoyles, and several mythological beings.

The Celtic Wind Castle of the East was connected with the color red, representing the dawn. In a traditional magickal circle, the candle in the East is yellow. To the Norse, the dwarf Austri held up the East end of the sky and ruled Air.

The ancient Mayans believed that the East was the red Bacab. In other Mexican cultures, the East was green and represented water.

Native American tribes had several designations for East, among them yellow and the eagle. The Navajo color was white, the Cheyenne and Zuni yellow, and the Spirit Keeper was called Wabun.

In the Enochian and Kabalistic traditions, the archangel Raphael ruled the East or Air, the Hebrew Quarter was Kedem (the front), and the Castle was colored red.

The Hindu Tattwas *Vayu* is a blue circle.

One ancient Chinese system of cardinal points believed that East was connected with the color green, wood, and the spring.

Air Element Characteristics

Direction: East.

Description: gaseous, vaporous matter, anything with an invisible gaseous form. In Welsh, *Breath*, meaning every wind, breeze, respiration, air.

Elemental Spirits: sylphs, zephyrs, and certain types of faeries. Pegasus, Arabian Buraq, Sleipnir, Phoenix, Firebird, Arabian Ruk, White Eagle of Zeus, Garuda, Djinn, Harpies, Griffin, Winged Serpent, gargoyles.

Color: yellow. Scots/Irish red.

Archangel: Raphael.

Ruler of the Element: Paralda.

Time: dawn or 6 a.m, and spring.

Plane: mental.

Senses: smell.

Property: hot and moist.

Power Animal of Light: falcon, griffin.

Power Animal of Dark: raven, bees.

Tattwas: *Vayu*, a blue circle.

Tarot Suit: wands. (Some writers list the East as swords. However, I feel that wands go with mental pursuits, while swords belong with activity.)

Kabalistic World: Yetzirah, Formative World.

Symbols: sky, wind, breezes, clouds, the breath, vibrations.

Astrological Signs: Gemini, Libra, Aquarius.

Personality Traits: Positive: optimism, joy, intelligence, mental quickness. Negative: frivolity, gossip, fickleness, bragging, inattention to responsibilities, lying.

Magickal Tools: wand, scepter, incense, creative visualization.

Ritual Work: business, legal problems, travel, gaining information and knowledge, logic, writing, locating the proper teachers, divination, creativity, healing nervous illnesses, plant growth, revealing the truth, finding lost objects.

The Elemental Spirits of Air

The traditional Elemental Spirits of Air are the sylphs and zephyrs. Their king is Paralda. However, many other beings are associated with the Element of Air in one manner or another. We can discover these by studying cultural histories and folktales.

Elemental Spirits of Air, like those of Fire, are notoriously unpredictable and difficult to control. The magician must know exactly what she or he wants from these beings. The first slip in concentration, and these Spirits are gone. They rarely cause trouble if they escape the control of a magician.

The forms of the Air Spirits are transparent to the point of being invisible most of the time. They are wispy, insubstantial creatures, who move rapidly from one place to another. The rapid parade of various thoughts through the human mind mimics the movements of Elemental Air Spirits. Except for holding onto storm patterns, the concentration powers of these beings are just as fleeting and changeable. The easiest magicks to work with the Elementals of Air are weather working, inspiration, or ideas. These beings take a remarkable interest in weather and its patterns.

Another interest of these Elementals is inspiration and the forming of ideas. They take a direct interest in the nebulous thought processes of the human mind. They have an unending supply of inspiration to give to those humans who ask. And they share this power freely. However, they are not interested in turning inspiration or ideas into a concrete, physical form. Their only interest lies in the formation of this energy through the mental processes.

If a magician knows the secrets of controlling certain of the Air Elementals, she or he can persuade them to give out enough energy to actually create a physical manifestation. However, it is best to combine all the Elements, instead of just using the Elemental Spirits of Air alone.

Air Faeries

This type of faery is very different from the Earth faeries and the fey. They live in the high mountainous regions or the deep deserts where the Element of Air moves freely and constantly with considerable force. Like the Elementals of Air, they have very insubstantial forms and are difficult to see. They blend with their surroundings to such an extent that they can move quite freely without any detection by human or animal. If seen in their natural state, they would appear as very pale, nearly devoid of color.

The air faeries attached to the greater mountains, such as the Himalayas, grow to be huge in size. They seem to slowly adjust to a size appropriate to the high places where they live. The ones of the deep deserts are thin and fluctuate in height as they ride the hot, sandy winds. None of these faeries willingly make contact with humans.

Air faeries rarely associate with their kin in other areas. They live solitary or in very small groups. They prefer the solitude of their chosen mountains or deserts to interaction with others. If one is in the high mountains or the deep, silent deserts with the winds blowing, you can hear the light, eerie, singing voices of the air faeries, carrying for miles on the turbulent breezes.

Magickal Uses: Freedom, travel, and swift changes in your life.

Arabian Buraq

The Arab cultures have many stories surrounding the Prophet Mohammed. One of these is about his magickal flying horse called Al Borak, Buraq, or Burak, depending upon the translation.

This unusual steed was said to have the body of a milk-white horse, a human head, and peacock tail. This image is found on ancient Persian miniatures. Stories say that one of its strides could outdistance human sight.

When it was time for Mohammed to leave earth, he rode this animal to Jerusalem. There, Buraq carried the Prophet to heaven with one mighty leap. Tradition says Buraq's hoof mark can still be seen in the rock from which it left the ground.

Magickal Uses: Moving from one level of the Otherworld to another while in meditation or trance.

Arabian Ruhk

In the Middle and Far East, there are many stories of giant magickal birds, besides the Phoenix. The Chinese had the *Fei Lie*; the Greeks, the White Eagle of Zeus; and the Persians, the *Simurgh*. The Arabs tell of the *Ruhk*. Sometimes the name of this gigantic bird is spelled *Roc*. It is vividly described in *The Arabian Nights*. The rook in chess was originally named the *ruhk*.

Whenever it flew, the ruhk was said to blot out the sun with its gigantic form. It fed entire full-grown elephants to its young. Each of its eggs was as large as 148 chicken eggs. Each egg was rounded like the dome of a mosque.

Every feather of the ruhk was as large as a palm frond, and its wing beats created lightning and windstorms.

Although some Arabic stories say that the ruhk never landed on earth, except for Mount Qaf, other tales mention that it lived in isolated places, especially islands in the Indian Ocean. Because the animals on these islands couldn't possibly feed a nesting pair of ruhks, these birds flew to Africa, India, and Arabic for food. A ruhk was capable of flying off with an elephant without a problem.

The Arabian Nights is a collection of stories, including "The Story of Sinbad the Voyager." This tale tells of several occasions when the Arab sailor encountered ruhks. Once he was marooned on an island in the Indian Ocean, where he hid behind a ruhk egg. When the mother ruhk came back to sit on the egg, Sinbad tied himself to one of her legs. In this manner, he flew off the island with the ruhk the next morning. When she landed in a steep-walled valley to hunt serpents, Sinbad cut himself loose and hid among the boulders. Later, he was rescued by merchants hunting diamonds. The ruhk's body and wings blotted out all the light shining into the valley when she flew away.

Another time when Sinbad was traveling with other men in a large ship, they stopped at an island where they killed and ate a young ruhk. When the angry parents returned, the sailors fled to their ship and cast off. The adult ruhks grasped huge boulders in their talons and dropped them onto the ship. They sunk the ship and killed everyone aboard, except Sinbad. He floated away to safety by clinging to the debris.

Magickal Uses: Protection.

Gargoyles

Long before their appearance in European Gothic art, gargoyles were known as grotesques in the Mediterranean area and as far back in history as ancient Rome and Greece. Statues of these Otherworld beings were originally found in grottoes and sacred caves. Later, under the Christian influence, gargoyles made their appearances as guardians on church roofs. Although presently associated with places such as Paris and old Europe, gargoyles also exist in American cities, as in New York and the Minneapolis-St. Paul area.

The name gargoyle comes from the Greek *gargarizein* (gargle) and the Latin *gurgulio* (gullet, windpipe, or trachea). Because depictions of these creatures were used as rainspouts, people naturally assume that is what their name means. Only magicians seem to make the deeper connection between gargoyles and the Otherworld. The trachea not only expels things, but draws in air. Ordinary air has always been considered filled with spiritual energy, available to those who know how to use it. The gargoyles' ability to charge the air with greater energy and change the negative into the positive places it in the role as an Air Elemental.

Although gargoyles are powerful protectors, the magician should be careful in how she or he uses them. These beings are capable of determining true motives of any human, and will turn negative magick back upon the magician if misused. They are often found at the dimensional doorways into the Otherworld.

These Elemental Spirits of Air also have the capability to drain away negative energies and influences that cause psychic rot and erosion in human lives. They soak up this type of energy, transform it into positive patterns, and return it to the psychic atmosphere. No Elemental actually lives in a statue representing it. However, the statue can be used as a touch-point between you and the Elementals on the astral plane. A gargoyle statue can be used as a receptacle for unhealthy, negative thoughts and feelings in your life. Simply place your hands on the statue and release the negative energy.

The manmade images of gargoyles reflect the various shapes they take. With some, their tongues are protruding, while others have one or two horns on their heads. Some have wings; some are gnawing on something. All of them are rather ugly. However, appearances can be deceiving compared to what gargoyles can do.

These Elemental Spirits are symbols of the world of psychic phenomena and human abilities to learn to use the psychic. They also are vital teachers of ancient spiritual mysteries and practices.

Magickal Uses: Developing the psychic, for protection, researching past lives, and companions on astral journeys and meditations.

Garuda

The *Mahabharata* of India describes this Elemental Spirit as the Bird of Life. As both the steed and servant of the god Vishnu, Garuda is considered to be one who destroys and creates all. He is portrayed with a human body and limbs, but with the head, wings, beak, and claws of a giant eagle. His body is golden, his wings red, and his face white. Garuda is also popular in Indo-China, Siam, Cambodia, and most of Southeast Asia.

Garuda is said to be the enemy of all serpents, and for a good reason. His mother *Vinata* (also the mother of the god Vishnu) and her sister Kadru (queen of the serpents) made a bet against each other about the color of the horses born from the churning of the Sea of Milk at creation. Kadru cheated so that she won and took Vinata and Garuda as her slaves.

Determined to win freedom for his mother and himself, Garuda went to steal some ambrosia from the gods. The ambrosia was protected by a fire barrier and venomous snakes. The bird-man killed the snakes, grabbed the ambrosia, and freed his mother. Vishnu was so impressed that he gave Garuda eternal life.

As a tireless enemy of snakes, he can sense the presence of any evil creatures. He also has the ability to track down and punish human offenders.

Magickal Uses: Dealing with radical life changes, for healing, and for protection from enemies.

Griffin

This enormous creature is half-bird and half-mammal. It has the wings, foreparts, front legs, and head of an eagle, and the rear-parts, hind paws, tail, and ears of a lion. Ancient writing says that the griffon is eight times larger than a lion and has the strength of 100 eagles. The beak and legs are golden with black talons, but it can appear in a number of different colors. It can be tawny to golden, pure white, or cream flecked with scarlet on the breast feathers. However, the griffins of Nemesis (goddess of retribution) were totally black and they are instruments of punishment. The griffin's young were hatched from eggs.

This intelligent Elemental Spirit was known in the Middle East, Greece, India, Turkey, Armenia, Syria, and Iraq. These countries are all semi-arid areas where huge deposits of gems once existed. The Assyrians called this being the "cloud-cleaving eagle," while Scythia knew it as the "Bird of Gold." In Mesopotamia, the griffin was portrayed with a crested head.

This being has very keen hearing and eyesight. It also has the ability to detect anything poisonous or full of negative energy. It guards the pathway to spiritual enlightenment. To symbolize this, the griffin is often pictured next to the Tree of Life.

Magickal Uses: New beginnings, gaining spiritual enlightenment, and learning to control your dark side.

Harpies

No one has ever been certain how many Greek harpies are loose in the world. The Greek stories only say that these are very large, predatory birds. They had a winged body like a vulture, the claws of an eagle, but the head and face of a woman. However, some sources call them winged women of ethereal beauty. The difference between being beautiful or ugly is only a breath apart among Elemental Spirits. The name "harpy" comes from the Greek word *harpyiai*, or snatchers, ravishers.

These Elemental Spirits of wind, storm, thunder, and lightning always give off a foul stench of evil when they appear. They make harsh, semi-human screams and have very large wings. They can be visible or invisible at will.

The Harpies have the mission of punishing or tormenting those who break spiritual laws. They create misery and disaster in life. It isn't possible to escape their punishment.

Magickal Uses: It isn't recommended that anyone work with these beings. Their energies are extremely difficult to control.

Jinn or Genie

The jinn (plural), or jinni (singular), made their way into the European language as the word "genie." These beings are found in Persian, North African, Egyptian, Syrian, Turkish, Arabian, and Muslim folklore, where they were said to be ugly demons with supernatural powers. Created out of smokeless fire before humans existed, the jinn are said to reveal themselves in the whirling sandstorms of the deep desert, or the Empty Quarter. However, they have the ability to be anywhere they wish, and in any form they wish.

The jinn are considered to be of four races: Earth, Air, Fire, and Water. Within each of these races, they live in seven tribes. Each tribe has a king, who controls it, and who is controlled by an angel.

Early Arabian beliefs stated that the jinn could be an inspiration for poets, mystics, and psychic readers. This gives the beings a dual nature, as they also take delight in punishing humans for any harm done to them, even if it is unintentional. Sometimes, jinn will haunt or inhabit a room or a specific building, driving out any humans who try to use that space. Certain Arabian manuscripts say that part of the jinn accepted Islam, while others did not.

Although usually invisible, the jinn can be called upon and used in magick by certain magicians, called *Muqarribun* in Arabic. King Solomon had a ring that he used to call up the jinn to aid his armies in battle, and to erect special buildings. Although nothing is recorded about the large stone in King Solomon's ring, some historians believe it was a diamond.

The jinn have bodies similar to those of humans. They need food, marry, have children, and die. They are not immortal, although they live for centuries. They can also intermarry or interbreed with humans. They have homes all over the earth, for use when they come to this plane of existence. Sometimes, these homes are in ancient ruins, graveyards, or other desolate places. However, their main homes are in Irem Zhat al Imad, which is on another level of reality. Irem itself exists in the Rub al Khali, or the Void between worlds.

The specially trained magician must enter an altered state of consciousness to visit Irem. There, the

Muqarribun can interact with and command the jinn by his or her magick. This type of magician can capture and enslave a jinni to do her or his bidding, or kill it. If enslaved, the magician may tie the jinni to a physical object, such as a piece of jewelry or the lamp mentioned in *The Arabian Nights*. King Solomon's famous ring may have been the "home" of a jinni. While enslaved or controlled, the jinni must do whatever the *Muqarribun* commands.

Magickal Uses: This being must be treated with respect and caution, and not called upon unless the magician is highly trained. The jinn will grant any wish, either good or evil.

Pegasus

This winged, white horse with the ability to fly sprang full-grown from the blood of Medusa when Perseus killed her. Pegasus immediately flew to Mount Helicon, where the Muses took him in. The Fountain of Hippocrene (the Moon-Horse spring) on Mount Helicon was dedicated to the Muses and tended by the Pegae, or water priestesses, who wore horse-masks. This cult may have originated in ancient Egypt, where the shrine of Osiris at Abydos had a sacred well called Pega.

Pegasus was so pure that he could fly straight to the gates of Olympus. He was considered to be beautiful, wise, and gentle. However, this winged horse also had a darker side. Very ancient Greek records tell of a female winged horse named Aganippe. She was associated with the goddess Demeter, and created destroying nightmares.

There are mythological hints that Aganippe was reborn in Pegasus.

Magickal Uses: Astral travel; inspiration; eloquence; journeys to the Otherworld for teaching; changing evil into good; gaining poetic inspiration.

Sleipnir

This eight-legged horse of cloud-gray is found in the Norse-Germanic tales. He was born from the union of the vicious Loki in horse-form and the giant stallion Svadilfari. He was associated with the god Odin or Wodan, and symbolized death and the journey to the Underworld. Hermod rode Sleipnir to the Underworld after the god Balder was slain by the mistletoe arrow. In Old Norse, this horse's name means "Slipper or Sliding One."

In his capacity as leader of the Wild Hunt, Odin rode Sleipnir through the night skies with his fierce band of warriors, who also rode cloud-gray horses. They rode over the mountains and through the forests, carrying off any humans they found. Farmers left the last sheaf of grain in the fields for the horses of the Wild Hunt, hoping that the Huntsman would pass them by.

The French knew the leader of the Wild Hunt as the Grand Huntsman of Fontainebleau. In England, the Wild Huntsman, who rode Sleipnir, gradually became known as Herne the Hunter. This strange antler-crowned being is said to still haunt Windsor Park, and occasionally ride the night skies.

Magickal Uses: To make astral contact with deceased loved ones and ancient ancestors, and on any journey to the Underworld.

Sylphs and Zephyrs

Paracelsus, the Swiss philosopher and ceremonial magician, was the first to record the Elemental Spirits connected with the four Elements. He got his information from very ancient sources no longer available to us.

The sylphs are slender female figures that ride and tumble through the winds like bubbles. They are graceful, happy creatures, unless there is a storm. Then, they become vicious beings of a wild, disheveled appearance and destructive nature.

The zephyrs are masculine Air Spirits, who command the winds. Usually, they ride the air currents with the sylphs, laughing and playing as they ride one wind to the end, and then leap onto another current. Like the dainty sylphs, the zephyrs change appearance and temperament when storms break and the winds howl.

Magickal Uses: Getting things to move in your life, making changes.

White Eagle of Zeus

The Greek god Zeus had a special messenger he often used: a beautiful, gigantic white eagle whose feathers glowed. This bird could move easily from one plane of existence to another and it communicated with the deities and humans alike by telepathy. Sometimes, by the order of Zeus, this eagle carried human passengers from one place to another. Its appearance signaled to magicians that an extremely important message from a Higher Source was on the way.

Magickal Uses: Telepathy, moving from one plane of existence to another during meditation, communing with spirit guides.

Winged Serpent

Many people are aware of the sacred winged serpent deity of ancient Egypt, known as Buto to the Greeks and Ua Zit to the Egyptians. However, ancient writers, such as Aristotle, Virgil, Ovid, Lucan, and Herodotus, recorded the existence of other winged serpents, or snakes. Most agreed that these serpents were found in the Arabian, Libyan, and Egyptian areas. Josephus wrote that it was not unusual for hordes of winged serpents to come from Libya to infest the lands along the Nile. Later, Cicero also recorded that, while on a journey into Egypt, he saw ibises killing and eating winged snakes there. These special creatures moved about by flying, not crawling, as ordinary snakes do.

Ancient Egyptian art shows these winged creatures as having either two or four wings. Some of their wings looked like those of bats, while others' resembled the feathered wings of birds. Tradition says that the winged serpents guarded frankincense trees. In Arabic, the words for snake, life, and teaching are all related.

Buto's material symbol was the uraeus (cobra) worn in a crown by the pharaoh. Her sacred books of great teachings were said to be in a crypt under Thoth's main temple at Hermopolis Magna in Upper Egypt. No one but the disciples of that temple were allowed to see and read these scrolls. The scrolls containing the wisdom of the god Thoth were also kept in this crypt. All these scrolls held great spiritual and magickal wisdom that was not taught, except to special students.

Magickal Uses: Protection; learning sacred spiritual teachings; gaining ancient knowledge through meditation or journeys into the Otherworld.

Meditations for the Air Element

Flying With the Elemental Spirits of Sylphs and Zephyrs

Sit in a comfortable chair with your hands in your lap and your feet flat on the floor. Make certain you will not disturbed by the telephone, someone at the door, pets, or any other people in the house. It may be helpful to play a CD of soft nature sounds, to mask any slight background noises. If you put each meditation on a tape, leave spaces in the appropriate places so that you have time to explore or listen to whoever is speaking to you.

Visualize a brilliant white light surrounding and penetrating your body. This is your protection throughout the meditation. Now, slowly begin to relax your body, beginning at the feet and ending at the head. During this time, breathe steadily and evenly. Breathe out all the negatives and troubles in your life. Breathe in the white light of healing and balance.

You are standing on top of a mountain. There are only a few trees in the very rocky area surrounding you. You feel the wind blowing against you, curling over the mountaintop as it continues its journey to far away places.

As you look around, you become aware that you can actually see the faint swirls of the wind as it moves past you. The outline is transparent except very pale blue edges around each current and whirl. You reach out with one hand into the wind. You see the wind flow around your hand, yet at the same time you feel energy entering your body from its touch.

As you freely allow the Air energy to course through your body, you notice movement at the edges of your vision. You stare at that area, knowing that something, someone is riding the winds and watching you. Within seconds, you see the faint bodies of Air faeries as they flit through the wind, directing Air energy into the few trees on the mountaintop. You send them thoughts that you will not harm them or their area. You feel the shy touch of welcome returning to you.

You walk farther out onto the mountaintop and sit on a boulder, watching the wind cur-

rents and their unusual, changing patterns. Suddenly, you feel the light touch of many hands on your body, and you float upward. As you look around, you see the slender bodies of the sylphs, happy smiles on their faces. With them, and grinning just as broadly, are the male zephyrs.

"Come, play with us," one of the sylphs says. "We will teach you to ride the winds and how Air energy can work for you. Let yourself fly free with the winds."

"Yes, come and play with us." A zephyr holds his position in front of you, bobbing up and down in the winds. "We will take you far across the country beyond. You will see how beautiful the land is, and feel at peace with yourself in the air."

As you, too, bob in the moving air currents, you decide to go with the sylphs and zephyrs as they travel far beyond on the winds. A zephyr takes one of your hands, and a sylph the other. Together, they pull you along the fast moving current of air until you learn how to move by yourself. You look down at the wondrous land patterns below, admiring the colors and patterns of the earth. The warm air against your body is soothing to your mind and spirit.

You soon see and feel other wind currents join and mingle with the one on which you ride.

You notice a slight difference in the Air energy from these mergers. The wind moves faster, but is not rough to move with. The mingled energy prickles against your skin, and makes you feel more alert as it soaks into your body.

Ahead, you see a tall range of mountains. The winds coming toward you from those mountains are not edged in blue as is the one you ride. They are edged in gray.

"Prepare!" one of the zephyrs shouts. "A change is coming!"

The sylphs and zephyrs show no fear as they approach the gray-tinted current coming directly at them. You feel safe in their company and continue to go with them.

As the two wind currents touch, you feel a solid bump, and find yourself staying in one place instead of moving forward. You watch the male zephyrs as they slowly merge into the oncoming current. They begin to change from their light-hearted forms into hulking, darker shapes with brilliantly glowing eyes. As the sylphs follow them, the female figures shapeshift from their dainty, smiling forms into strong women with long flowing hair that shoots out sparks. Their little hands grow long nails, and their faces become grim.

You feel the coldness of the oncoming current as it forces itself into the warm air around you.

You notice that similarly grim sylphs and zephyrs ride this new wind that seems charged with negative particles. The two groups meet, swirling around each other in a strange dance.

The air swiftly forms into black clouds that growl and shove, as they bump against each other. You hold yourself back from this fast forming storm so you can observe without being in the unpleasant atmosphere of the storm itself.

Lightning suddenly flashes from the long, tangled hair and the talon-like nails of the dancing sylphs. The grim zephyrs grab the lightning flashes, infuse them with greater energy, and hurl them through the black clouds toward the earth below.

You realize the extreme negative and positive powers of the Element of Air and the Elemental Spirits that are attached to it. You feel knowledge on how to use these powers sink into your mind.

You feel that you have seen enough of the sylphs and zephyrs, how they can change forms, and the powers they can call upon. You decide to return to your body.

You think of your physical body. You slide down the tunnel of light into that body. You open your eyes. The meditation is finished.

Flying to the Temple of the Moon

Sit in a comfortable chair with your hands in your lap and your feet flat on the floor. Make certain you will not disturbed by the telephone, someone at the door, pets, or any other people in the house. It may be helpful to play a CD of soft nature sounds, to mask any slight background noises. If you put each meditation on a tape, leave spaces in the appropriate places so that you have time to explore or listen to whoever is speaking to you.

Visualize a brilliant white light surrounding and penetrating your body. This is your protection throughout the meditation. Now, slowly begin to relax your body, beginning at the feet and ending at the head. During this time, breathe steadily and evenly. Breathe out all the negatives and troubles in your life. Breathe in the white light of healing and balance.

You are walking along a path leading up into a grove of trees on a mountainside. It is night. A full moon shines brightly overhead. You move quickly through the trees until you emerge in a small clearing beyond. In the center of this clearing you see a small, glowing, white, marble temple, its round shape held up by columns that form open sides to the building.

You walk up the two steps into this temple. In the center you see a spring that bubbles up into a basin, and then runs off one side to create a small stream. The stream disappears into the trees at the far side of the clearing. You kneel down and, cupping your hands, bring the cold, clear water to your mouth to drink.

You heard the snort of a horse and the stamp of its foot behind you. Turning, you see Pegasus standing in the moonlight, his white coat glowing bright in the night. His great feathered winds fan the air in impatience. You walk down the marble steps and mount this fantastic creature without fear.

Pegasus gives a mighty leap toward the sky, his wings flapping to lift him into the air. You hold tightly to his mane, amazed at the rapidly retreating scenery below you, as Pegasus heads upward toward the full moon. Soon the earth is only a blue and white ball far below you in the dark night sky.

Within a short time, Pegasus lands on the moon, his hooves raising a small cloud of dust. A few yards away is a larger duplicate of the temple you found in the clearing. This time you can see several women seated on chairs inside the temple.

Filled with curiosity, you go to the temple and stand in the circle of seated women. They tell you that they are the Muses, the powers that intensify or give gifts of talents to humans. You see a tall mirror hanging from one of the pillars, but its surface is black instead of reflective.

"What talents do you wish to grow stronger?" one of the Muses asks.

Your reply may have to do with your job or a hobby.

"We will send many opportunities your way to strengthen these talents," the Muse says. "And you will be taught by teachers in the astral realm when you sleep."

The women all point to the tall, black mirror. "Look closely within," another Muse says. "You will see a past life that directly affects your life now."

You walk to the mirror and stare into it. At first, there are only flickers of movement on the black surface. Then, you clearly see the lifetime that affects your present life. You see your interactions with people you know now. You realize what steps you must take and what you must learn to make your present life better and to resolve any negative karmic ties.

As you turn away from the mirror, you see that the Muses have disappeared, leaving behind their gilded chairs. Outside the temple, Pegasus stamps his front hoof, as if impatient to be on his way back to the earth. You mount the winged horse, and he leaps skyward in one great bound.

The flight back toward earth gives you a marvelous view of the blue marble-like image of the planet ahead. Suddenly, Pegasus gives a mighty twitch. *You fall off the horse's back and find yourself falling back toward your physical body.*

You think of your physical body. You slide down the tunnel of light into that body. You open your eyes. The meditation is finished.

Meeting a Jinni

Sit in a comfortable chair with your hands in your lap and your feet flat on the floor. Make certain you will not be disturbed by the telephone, someone at the door, pets, or any other people in the house. It may be helpful to play a CD of soft nature sounds, to mask any slight background noises. If you put each meditation on a tape, leave spaces in the appropriate places so that you have time to explore or listen to whoever is speaking to you.

Visualize a brilliant white light surrounding and penetrating your body. This is your protection throughout the meditation. Now, slowly begin to relax your body, beginning at the feet and ending at the head. During this time, breathe steadily and evenly. Breathe out all the negatives and troubles in your life. Breathe in the white light of healing and balance.

You are standing in the desert at the edge of very ancient ruins. Walls are still standing, giv-

ing shade from the afternoon sun. You quickly get into the shade of a wall because the sun is so hot. You sit on one of the fallen blocks of stone. This sitting position protects you from the hot desert wind that comes from deep within the Empty Quarter. As you listen to the whistling wind through the ruins, you hear very faint voices within the wind. They are so soft it is impossible to make any sense of the words. Every so often you detect the sound of laughter among the words. Tiny whirlwinds dance through the ruins and out again into the vast expanse of the desert.

You look around at the ruins and wonder what people once lived here and what this city looked like. Another tiny whirlwind speeds close to you and out of the ruins. You stare down at the marks of its passing left in the fine sand. Sunlight momentarily glints off something unearthed by the wind. You reach down and pick up the object. In your hand lies a very old ring with a large stone set into the gold. You rub it vigorously against your clothes to get rid of some of the grime. Then you slip it onto your finger and admire it.

The air before you shivered as if a doorway suddenly opened. There stands a very large jinni. He is dressed in loose Persian trousers with a sash around his muscled waist. His hair is one long, thick strand of black hair growing from the top of his head. He folds his arms and stares down at you.

"Who are you, human, that you call me?" The jinni's voice is deep and rumbling.

You glance down at the ring as it twists a little on your finger. You touch it with your other hand and feel the power that holds the jinni before you.

"Respect me, and I will respect you," you tell the jinni. "I ask only for your teaching about the Elements and the Elemental Spirits who are connected with each Element. I seek true knowledge."

The jinni raises one black eyebrow in surprise as he continues to stare at you.

"A human who seeks true knowledge? That is a rarity," the jinni says. "Do you not want fame or riches?"

You shake your head. "Knowledge is worth more than fame or riches," you answer.

The jinni laughs loudly. Then he points his finger at a block of stone, and it speeds across the ruins to provide the jinni with a seat. He sits on the stone before you.

"I will make you a bargain, human. I will teach you about the Elements and their Spirits. However, you will not remember everything when you return to your body. Some of what I say will return to your mind while you sleep. More will make itself remembered from time to time, as you are capable of understanding the knowledge."

The jinni begins to talk to you, speaking of long forgotten knowledge of the four Elements. He tells you in detail about the Elemental Spirits connected to each Element. He talks for a long time. You may ask him any questions you wish.

"This is enough at this time," the jinni finally says. "I will teach you more when you sleep. And you may return here at any time to speak with me."

"Thank you," you tell the jinni. "You have been most helpful."

The jinni outlines a door in the air with one finger. You walk through the nearly invisible door and find yourself sliding into your physical body.

You think of your physical body. You slide down the tunnel of light into that body. You open your eyes. The meditation is finished.

Visiting the Hidden Temple of Wisdom

Sit in a comfortable chair with your hands in your lap and your feet flat on the floor. Make certain you will not be disturbed by the telephone, someone at the door, pets, or any other people in the house. It may be helpful to play a CD of soft nature sounds, to mask any slight background noises. If you put each meditation on a tape, leave spaces in the appropriate places so that you have time to explore or listen to whoever is speaking to you.

Visualize a brilliant white light surrounding and penetrating your body. This is your protection throughout the meditation. Now, slowly begin to relax your body, beginning at the feet and ending at the head. During this time, breathe steadily and evenly. Breathe out all the negatives and troubles in your life. Breathe in the white light of healing and balance.

You stand on the stone pavement before the Temple of Thoth in ancient Egypt. You know you are in the old city of Hermopolis Magna in Upper Egypt, many centuries ago. You admire the stone building and the brightly painted pictures around the open door. You walk into the temple and are met by a priest and a priestess, both dressed in the white clothing of ancient times.

"What do you desire here, Pilgrim?" the priest asks.

"I wish to read the ancient scrolls of Ua Zit and Thoth," you tell him. "I wish to learn all I can of the sacred and magickal knowledge from ancient times."

The priestess steps forward and puts one hand on your chest over your heart. She looks into your eyes with her dark eyes. You feel her reach into your mind for the truth.

"You speak the truth," she finally says. "You may pass and become a student of this Temple of Wisdom."

The priest and priestess lead the way through the main hall of the temple into a corridor. The walls of this corridor are painted with colorful scenes from the stories of the cobra goddess and the ibis-headed Thoth, the god of learning and wisdom. Soon the corridor ends in a locked door with an armed guard standing beside it.

As you approach, the guard unlocks the door and salutes the priest and priestess. You follow the two through the door and down a long flight of stairs. You realize that you are very deep under the main temple. Soon the stairs end at another door.

"This is a very sacred place," the priestess says softly, as the priest opens the door and walks into the lighted room beyond. "Here you will learn much forgotten knowledge of the Ancient Ones."

You go into the crypt and see that shelves of carefully rolled and tied scrolls line all the walls. In the center of the room is a gilded table with a cushioned chair by it.

"This scroll begins the learning," the priest says as you sit at the table. He lays a scroll before you.

"Study as long as you wish," the priestess adds. "I will come to return you to your world when enough time has passed. One cannot learn everything in these scrolls at one time."

She smiles as she and the priest leave the room, closing the door behind them.

You untie the scroll and roll it out on the table. As you look down at the hieroglyphs, they change into a language you can read. Fascinated by the old knowledge you find on Elemental Spirits, you read the scroll completely.

You look up to find the winged cobra hanging in the air before you. As you stare at her, she tells you things that you need to do to improve your spiritual growth. As quickly as she appeared, the winged serpent blinks out of sight.

You roll and tie the scroll and return it to its empty place on the shelf. You take another one to the table. You read for quite some time.

The priestess suddenly appears at your side. "Come," she says. "It is time for you to return to your time."

You roll and tie the scroll, and then put it back on the shelf. You follow the priestess to the door. As you step through the door, she turns and lightly taps you on the center of your forehead. You whirl out across time and return to your physical body.

You think of your physical body. You slide down the tunnel of light into that body. You open your eyes. The meditation is finished.

Magickal Uses of Air Energy

Remember, working with the Air Elemental Spirits can be difficult. You must hold your concentration on what you are doing at all times. In this way, you will hold the attention of these easily-distracted beings.

If you need to substitute oils, herbs, incense, or candle colors, see the Appendix.

Spell for Legal Problems

✦   one purple candle

✦   one black candle

✦   any papers concerning your legal problem

✦   cinnamon incense

✦   If you want to roll the candles in oil and herbs, choose from the lists in Chapter 4.

Timing: best done during the waning moon or on a new moon.

Spell: Light the incense. Use a sharp object to scratch the word "success" into the purple candle, and the word "justice" into the black candle. Set the two candles far enough apart to lay your legal papers between them. Light the candles.

Concentrate on the purple candle, and chant:

> *I ask that success in this case be mine,*
> *Aided by the Spirits of Air divine.*
> *The power of justice is not blind,*
> *A generous outcome will be mine.*

Concentrate on the black candle, and chant:

All barriers and walls come tumbling down,
Negativity dissipates all around.
The powers of Air have set me free.
How I wish, so shall it be.

Look at the purple candle, blinking when necessary, and concentrate on success in the legal matter. Keep concentrating for five minutes. Then put out both candles. Repeat this spell for five minutes each day until the candles are burned up.

Spell to Reveal the Truth

✧   one blue candle
✧   one white candle
✧   carnation incense
✧   small bowl of water
✧   clear quartz crystal

Timing: during the waxing moon or on the full moon.

Spell: Place the two candles side by side near the back of your altar or working space. Light the candles and the incense. Hold the crystal between your hands, and chant:

Elementals of Air, join with me
That truth will be revealed to me.
I know it is within your power
To help me in this troubled hour.

Gently place the crystal into the bowl of water. Take the bowl in both hands and say:

Like the Elementals of Air, my breath shall be,
As powerful as the winds and breeze.
All disguises and clouds are blown away.
All opposition gone. Only truth will stay.

Blow gently three times into the water, while concentrating on the question of truth you want answered. Be prepared to accept this truth when it is revealed, even if it is not what you might have wished it to be.

Leave the candles to burn out. Then dispose of the remaining wax.

At least once a day, blow gently three times into the water, while mentally asking for the truth. Repeat this for seven days. At the end of this time, remove the crystal from the water. Pour the water onto your plants or outside.

Spell to Help With Divination

✦　　one white or gold candle
✦　　honeysuckle incense
✦　　moonstones or brown stones
✦　　tarot cards or other divinatory devices

Timing: any time you do a reading.

Spell: Put the candle to the left of your working space. Place the moonstones or brown stones near it. Light the candle and the incense. Run both hands through the incense smoke to purify them.

Place your power hand on your divinatory tool, and say:

By the powers of both moon and sun,
My journey toward truth has now begun.
By power of Elements fourfold,
Only truth shall I behold.

Lay out the cards, or cast the stones, for the reading.

Spell to Heal Nervousness

- ✧ one magenta candle
- ✧ lavender incense
- ✧ a photo of the ill person, if possible
- ✧ a small piece of paper with the name of the person who needs healing written on it
- ✧ metal bowl or cauldron

Timing: best done on a full moon. However, this spell can be worked at any time there is a need.

Spell: Put the candle to the middle of the back of your altar. Light the candle and incense. Place the bowl or cauldron in front of the candle. Lay the paper with the name beside the cauldron.

Take the photo in both hands and look at it. If you don't have a photo, look at the paper bearing the person's name. Concentrate as long as you can on that person's unbalanced emotions. See these emotions as a lake. Every time you see a roughness in the water, mentally smooth it out. When the lake is as smooth as you can make it, lay aside the photo. Fold the name paper in half, and say:

Only calm and balance shall be with you,
        _____ (person's name).

Light the paper from the candle and drop it into the cauldron.

Put out the candle. You may need to repeat this spell seven or nine times, once a day, until the power begins to have an effect on the sick person.

Powering Air Amulets and Talismans

The Elemental Spirits of Air may be represented by a charm of a cloud, rainbow, or mountain. Representatives of Air also can be a jinn (genie) or a winged Pegasus. Leave the charm or charms on a crystal cluster overnight to empower them.

Talismans of Air can help you with mental acuity and forming ideas for a project.

Power Animals

Statues, pictures, or charms that represent the Power Animals can be used to add their special energy to any spells. The griffin is a powerful guardian entity that can cause new beginnings, bring enlightenment, and help you control your dark side. The raven has long been a sacred, even feared, bird in many cultures. Although a scavenger on the battlefields, the raven is also very cunning. It can help to absorb negative thoughts and actions directed at you.

To empower these symbols, hold or touch each one while saying the proper chant:

Griffin of Light, guardian and guide,
I ask that your powers in this symbol abide.

Raven of Dark, listen to me.
Absorb all negativity.

Stone Elixirs for Air Elementals

Make stone elixirs using chalcedony, moonstone, jade, watermelon tourmaline, and clear quartz crystal. (See the instructions for elixirs on pages 58-60.) Chalcedony helps to see through illusions. Moonstone is valuable when using tarot cards or other divinatory methods. Jade elixir aids whenever you need help in a court case. Watermelon tourmaline helps to heal and calm people, while clear quartz crystal will lead you to the truth in any situation. Remember to label each bottle.

Hold each jar in your hands and use the chant for appropriate stone.

Chalcedony

This stone comes in blue, gray, purple, green, pink, and white colors. It helps to see through illusions, repels negative vibrations, cleanses the aura, and stabilizes the emotions.

Into this water pour your powers,
Reveal illusions, repel negativity,
Cleanse all auras that you touch.
As I do will, so shall it be.

Moonstone

Although this stone is mostly transparent, misty, and iridescent, it can also be in the colors of peach, brown, pink, pale green, and gray. It breaks up rigid ideas, opens communication with others, unmasks secret enemies, and is a great aid in foretelling the future.

> *As luminescent as the moon,*
> *As powerful as the moon on tide,*
> *Your energies shall pour out*
> *And within this water shall abide.*

Jade

As with many stones, jade comes in yellow, red, black, blue, gray, lavender, orange, pink, white, and the popular green. It will drain off excessive emotions or energy when rubbed as a worry stone. It also helps with karmic issues, past lives, and interpreting dreams.

> *All worries drained, all karma gone,*
> *The secret of past lives revealed.*
> *Oh stone of dreams and forecasts strong,*
> *Into this elixir you are sealed.*

Watermelon Tourmaline

This stone is a mixture of pink and green. It is excellent for removing imbalances or confusion in life as well as healing.

> *Bright colored stone of balance,*
> *Healing and much happiness,*
> *This elixir water, clear and pure,*
> *May you willingly seal and bless.*

Clear Quartz Crystal

Rock crystal is colorless and transparent. It usually is shaped like a rod with a pointed tip on at least one end. An all-purpose stone, it can also reveal the truth, enhance psychic powers, change your luck, destroy negative energies, and amplify spell energy.

> *Clear stone of much power great,*
> *There is nothing you cannot do.*
> *Those whom this elixir blesses,*
> *May have their life forces all renewed.*

Gift to the Air Elementals

As a gift to the Elemental Spirits of Air, get a bottle of bubble solution. Blow, or wave into existence, colorful bubbles that float away on the winds. While you do this, think about the Air Elementals. Mentally tell them the bubbles are your gift to them. Enjoy yourself while doing this. Feel as light and free as the air that moves around you.

Confidence Paper Spell

- ✧ a small circle cut from yellow construction paper
- ✧ an orange candle
- ✧ one whole clove bud
- ✧ frankincense oil
- ✧ a pencil or pen

Timing: during a waxing moon, or on a full moon.

Spell: Scratch your first name onto the orange candle with a nail or knife. Put it in a safe place, and light it. Say:

I seek changes in myself and my life.

Using the pencil or pen, write your full name in the middle of the yellow circle of paper. Around the edges of the circle, write "I stand tall in confidence. I am of value."

Anoint the center where your name is with one drop of frankincense oil. Fold the circle in half, and then in half again. Make two small holes at the rounded edge of the folded circle. Push the clove bud stem into these holes so that it keeps the paper closed. Hold the paper lightly in your power hand and say:

> *Elementals of Air, so joyous and strong,*
> *Fill my mind with your powers great,*
> *So my confidence grows and expands.*
> *To make myself better is my fate.*

Put the folded circle under your pillow and sleep with it there for at least one full month.

Leave the orange candle to burn out. Dispose of the remaining wax.

Soul Mate Heart, Part 2

On the red paper heart you made in Chapter 1(the one that will describe your soul mate for whom you are seeking) write out all the mental qualities you would like to find in a mate, such as intelligence and positive abilities to work. Close the heart on the folds you made the last time.

Hold the folded paper against your chest in the area of your own heart and chant:

> *Like minds call to like, soul mate dear.*
> *No conflicts shall be allowed here.*
> *Accord makes us a happy pair,*
> *Our strong love will make us care,*
> *For each other permanently.*
> *This is our will. So shall it be.*

Put the soul mate paper on your altar or in a safe place where no one will be handling it.

THE ELEMENT OF FirE

Like Fire, be fully alive in
body, mind, and spirit.

The Element of Fire is one of the most difficult Elements to understand and use. It is characterized as brilliance, burning matter, or heated or hot material. In Welsh, the word *Uvel*, symbolizes heat, fire, and light. Fire is insubstantial in character, but has the power to transform the appearance of most objects. Physically, it changes the molecular structure of an object into smoke, ashes, or particles that become part of other Elements. Spiritually, it purifies the astral and spiritual bodies, clears out Traditionally, the Elemental Spirits of Fire are the salamanders and firedrakes. Salamanders are an astral, lizard-like creature that have the power to endure fire withour harm. The firedrake is a small type of fire-breathing dragon. However, there are several other beings that are also connected with the Elemental Spirits of Fire. These are described on pages 118–123.

The tarot suit associated with Fire is swords. Some books list wands for the South and Fire. However, wands are a mental tool, while swords are for action and energy.

The Celtic Wind Castle for the South was white for the heat of noon. To the Norse, the dwarf *Sudhri* was in the South and represented Fire.

The Mayans believed the color of South was yellow. Other ancient Mexican cultures used blue for this direction.

One Native American idea was that the South was red and was connected with the mouse. The Spirit Keeper was named *Shawnodese*. To the Navajo, the South was blue, but, to the Zuni, the Southern color was red.

To the Enochian and Kabalistic magicians, the direction South was represented by the archangel Michael, and the Castle was white. In Hebrew studies, the South was *Yamin*, or to the right hand.

The Hindu Tattwas *Tijas* for the South was a red triangle.

One Chinese directional system said that the South was red, and connected with Fire and the summer.

Fire Element Characteristics

Direction: South (North in the Southern Hemisphere).

Description: brilliance, burning matter, or heated or hot material; in Welsh, *Uvel*, or heat, fire, or light.

Elemental Spirits: salamanders, firedrakes, and the consciousness of the flames.

Color: green; Scots/Irish, white.

Archangel: Michael.

Ruler of the Element: Djinn.

Time: noon and summer.

Plane: spiritual.

Senses: sight.

Property: hot and dry.

Power Animal of Light: horse, unicorn.

Power Animal of Dark: bull, crow, raven.

Tattwas: *Tijas*, a red triangle.

Tarot Suit: swords.

Kabalistic World: Atziluth, or the Archetypal World.

Symbols: fire, lightning, volcanoes, rainbow, the sun, stars, and blood.

Astrological Signs: Aries, Leo, Sagittarius.

Personality Traits: Positive: enthusiasm, activity, courage, daring, willpower, and leadership. Negative: hate, jealousy, fear, anger, ego, and contentiousness.

Magickal Tools: candles, incense burner, images, burned herbs, and burned requests on paper.

Ritual Work: power, physical freedom, change, passion, sexuality, energy, authority, confidence, success, personal fulfillment, and destruction of negative energies.

The Elemental Spirits of Fire

The Elemental Spirits of Fire are often connected with the sun in many ancient cultures and magickal systems. Their traditional king is Djinn. Although this name links the king of Fire with the jinn, I feel that the jinn belong more with Air than with Fire.

Fire Spirits are extremely unpredictable and easily can get out of a magician's control. They are the most likely to cause physical harm should this happen. I do not recommend that magicians work directly with the Fire Elementals unless they have had years of training.

Although they have no consistent physical form, their psychic and spiritual energies are necessary for the life and motive of both manifestations of spell work and human astral and spiritual bodies.

Alsvidr and Arvakr

In the Old Norse language, *Alsvidr* meant "very quick," and *Arvakr* meant "early awake." These two beings were supernatural horses that pulled the chariot of the sun through the skies. Because of her beauty and her father's boasting, the Norse gods made the girl *Sol* responsible for driving the chariot and controlling these fiery Elementals. They created the sun from a spark out of Muspellheim, and hooked this celestial orb to the back of the chariot.

Magickal Uses: They are used for finding your path in life and learning to handle stress and pressure.

Chimera

The word Chimera, also spelled Chimaera, originated from the Greek *chimaira* (she-goat), which is also related to the word *cheimon* (winter). Today, this word is used to mean an illusion or a fabrication of the mind.

This Elemental was associated with the cultures of the Mediterranean and Near East. Old stories say she was born to Typhon and Echidna. Originally, she was portrayed as having the front part of a goat and a the tail of a dragon. She also had three heads: goat, lion, and dragon. By Medieval times in Europe, the chimera was shown with a goat's head growing from the middle of her back and breathing fire.

Magickal Uses: A very dangerous being, the chimera should only be called upon as a last resort. She can hide your fears from others. Working with this Elemental Spirit is not recommended except for those who are highly trained.

Firedrakes

Firedrakes are very small members of the dragon family. They are not often longer than 4 or 5 inches. They prefer to spend as much time as they can in actual physical flames. However, if befriended, firedrakes will stay around a house or a person whether there is a fire or not. During spell work, it is not unusual for a firedrake to sit on the altar and stare at, or play with, the flame of a candle. If they play by swooping down and flying through the flame, it will lean to the side or make strange wavering movements. Being Elementals of Fire, firedrakes will react negatively to outbursts of temper or violence.

Magickal Uses: Astral guides into the Otherworld, Firedrakes are good for, protection and help with spell work.

Fire Faeries

This particular type of faery is seldom recognized unless one pays special attention to candle flames, incense coals, fireplaces, and campfires. It is rarely, if ever, seen in other places. These faeries are about 3 inches tall and do not wear clothing. They have bright red or yellow hair, very pale skin, and glittering eyes.

Fire faeries particularly love to dance in candle flames. Their wild dances are composed of high-kicking, twisting, and leaping steps. If they wish, they can communicate with you by making the flame turn to one side or the other, for yes or no answers. They are not afraid of humans because of their connection with the Element of Fire. However, like all Fire Elementals, they are aloof and tricky to handle. Still, you can attract them and obtain their help by frequently lighting several candles in a room, or on your altar during spell work. They are the easiest and safest of the Fire Elementals with which to work.

Magickal Uses: Fire faeries help with gaining a wish or desire, divination, mirror or stone scrying, and shapeshifting.

Hati and Skoll

These very dangerous Norse giant wolves are connected to the sun and the moon. *Hati*, which means "despiser or hater," is said to run before the chariot of the sun, while chasing the moon. The wolf *Skoll*, which means "mockery," runs before the chariot of the moon and chases the sun. At *Ragnarok*, or the Norse belief in the last battle that ends the world, these wolves will catch and devour the celestial bodies. The magician must take great precautions when calling upon these wolves.

Magickal Uses: Hati and Skoll aid in retribution for persecution and harassment.

Salamanders

The word salamander comes from the Greek word *salambe*, which means fireplace. Today, the name salamander has been transferred to a small newt that lives in wet areas, the complete opposition of the original salamander.

Medieval descriptions of the Fire salamanders are similar to the appearance to the black and yellow lizards that live in damp places in Europe, however, the Fire Elemental lives in the midst of flames, especially volcanoes and lava. Paracelsus wrote that they could also be found in St. Elmo's Fire and the small balls of light that appear during storms. When incense is burned, sometimes you will see tiny salamanders curling with the smoke.

Ancient magicians warned their students against trying to work with Fire salamanders because they are extremely dangerous and difficult to contact. Once called, they are also notoriously difficult to dismiss. There are no common grounds of thinking between these Elemental Spirits and humans.

Magickal Uses: Working with salamanders is NOT recommended.

Thunderbirds

Stories of the Thunderbird are found among the Native American tribes. However, there are hints that there is more than one of this type of being. It is a huge bird, connected with thunder and lightning, and considered to be very sacred. It lives above the clouds. Its flashing eyes created lightning, and its great wings produce thunder when they move.

The perpetual enemy of this Elemental Spirit is all evil. The Thunderbird is never surprised by the appearance of evil because it has highly tuned senses that give warning.

Intelligent magicians never invoke the Thunderbird. They know it will appear on its own will or not.

Magickal Uses: Thunderbirds are the enemy of all evil.

Vivasvat

The Hindus tell of a great seven-headed sun horse, whose name was *Vivasvat*. Shapeshifting into human form, this Elemental married Saranya and became the father of the twins Yama (king of the dead) and his sister Yami. Because of Vivasvat's terrible heat, Saranya created a simulacrum of herself and then shapeshifted into a mare and fled. When the sun horse begat Manu on the simulacrum, he realized that he had been tricked. He hunted until he found his wife. He shapeshifted into a great stallion and sired the Asvins, or horse-men, through her.

Each of the heads of Vivasvat represents one of the seven chakras in the astral body of humans. It is important that the magician keep her or his chakras cleaned and balanced.

Magickal Uses: Vivasvat aids in enlightenment and shapeshifting.

Fire Meditations

Meeting Fire Elementals

Sit in a comfortable chair with your hands in your lap and your feet flat on the floor. Make certain you will not be disturbed by the telephone, someone at the door, pets, or any other people in the house. It may be helpful to play a CD of soft nature sounds, to mask any slight background noises. If you put each meditation on a tape, leave spaces in the appropriate places so that you have time to explore or listen to whoever is speaking to you.

Visualize a brilliant white light surrounding and penetrating your body. This is your protection throughout the meditation. Now, slowly begin to relax your body, beginning at the feet and ending at the head. During this time, breathe steadily and evenly. Breathe out all the negatives and troubles in your life. Breathe in the white light of healing and balance.

You are standing at the base of a high, snow-covered mountain. You see a cloud of steam and vapor coming from the top of the mountain. On each side of you stands one of your spiritual guardians. They will remain with you at all times to protect and guide you, to answer any questions you may have.

The guardians lead you among the boulders and stunted trees at the foot of the mountain until you see a dark slit among the stones. One of your guides creates a small ball of brilliant light and sends it floating into the cave, illuminating the path. You follow it into the darkness.

You and your companions move swiftly down the twisting tunnel. The farther you go, the warmer the air becomes. Gradually, a red glow shines on the tunnel walls from some place ahead of you. At last, you find yourself standing on a wide ledge looking into a huge vaulted dome of a cave. The floor of this inner cave is a rippling, bubbling sea of molten lava. You know that you are in the heart of the mountain, and that this mountain is a volcano.

Your guides immediately surround you with protection against the great heat. They also reassure you that you will not be harmed in any way by the lava or any creatures you may find here.

As you follow your guides out onto the lava, something swoops down and settles on your shoulder. It is a small firedrake. Its skin is a beautiful blending of red, orange, and yellow. A tiny spurt of flame shoots from its mouth when it yawns. When you look back at the boiling lava, you see several groups of these tiny dragons diving into the hot lake, floating on the moving surface, and shooting back into the air again. These groups fly together like a flock of birds, turning in unison and filling the air with high pitched squeaks. Some are perched on small rock ledges along the sides of the volcanic dome.

A flock of firedrakes swarms around you. You begin to understand that they can communicate telepathically with you. You feel their vibrations brush against your skin and recognize the various energies of the Element of Fire. You feel your inner spark of divine fire respond to the energies of the primal fire around you, filling you with energy for action and a determination to expand your spiritual path. You communicate with the firedrakes for a few moments before moving on with your companions. The one firedrake remains on your shoulder, nestled close to your ear.

"Look down and around you," one of your guides says, pointing to the lava beneath your feet.

As you look down into the churning lava, you see hundreds of lizard-like creatures swimming in the molten rock as fish in a turbulent sea. Some of them are nearly a foot long, while others are smaller than your hand. They are fire salamanders. Like chameleons, their skin changes to match the shifting colors of the lava, making it difficult for you to keep them in sight for long. As you squat down to look at them closer, you feel their fire vibrations clearly. They emit more primitive, wild, and unpredictable auras than the firedrakes. You get no feeling of welcome or recognition from these beings.

"We will now show you other kinds of fire and the Elementals that inhabit those places." One of your guides takes your hand. The firedrake on your shoulder hisses loudly and flies away. Your companions and you suddenly leave the fiery mountain.

You find yourself streaking through the black night sky. To one side, you see the gigantic wolf Hati loping after the moon as it spins around the Earth. On the other side, you notice the matching wolf Skoll racing after the sun as it moves through the solar system. Your companions continue to lead you farther from the earth, until you see a round ball of fire with a streaming tail ahead of you.

"This comet will introduce you to similar, yet different, Fire Elementals," your guide says.

Within seconds you are standing on the comet's fiery surface of slowly burning rock. You see hundreds of Fire salamanders crawling through the flames, walking unharmed over heated stones that would destroy anything they touched. These salamanders look slightly different than the ones you saw inside the volcano. They have thicker bodies and glowing eyes. Their vibrations are also different, in that they feel far more primitive and destructive than others of their kind.

Flying in and out of the comet's fiery tail are several large dragons, their red and gold hued scales glistening like gems in the heat of the fire. When a small piece of the comet cracks off the main body and falls away into the black sky, one of these dragons veers off to snap it up as if it were food.

"Hold your hand close to the comet's surface," a guide suggests.

You kneel and hold both hands about a foot above the surface. The raw, primal energy nearly knocks you over. You reach out again. The fire flowing over and around your hands and body are uncontrollable.

"If you tap into a tiny particle of the Fire Element," your guide says, "you can add needed energy and life to any spell or ritual. Draw that Fire from fireplaces, candles, or firedrakes, though. Never try to control the Fire of volcanoes, comets, the stars, or the sun, for that energy is beyond the power of human control."

Your guides quickly take you in a blurred rush through the sky back to earth. Now you are standing beside a campfire burned down to coals. You become aware of very tiny salamanders and firedrakes in this fire as well. The salamanders leave you with a distinct impression that you should not call upon them. Even the more friendly firedrakes seem less personal and more dangerous than any other Elemental Spirits you have encountered.

You nod a farewell to your guides. You think of your physical body and streak back toward it.

You think of your physical body. You slide down the tunnel of light into that body. You open your eyes. The meditation is finished.

Working With Fire Elementals for Spiritual Growth

Sit in a comfortable chair with your hands in your lap and your feet flat on the floor. Make certain you will not be disturbed by the telephone, someone at the door, pets, or any other people in the house. It may be helpful to play a CD of soft nature sounds, to mask any slight background noises. If you put each meditation on a tape, leave spaces in the appropriate places so that you have time to explore or listen to whoever is speaking to you.

Visualize a brilliant white light surrounding and penetrating your body. This is your protection throughout the meditation. Now, slowly begin to relax your body, beginning at the feet and ending at the head. During this time, breathe steadily and evenly. Breathe out all the negatives and troubles in your life. Breathe in the white light of healing and balance.

You are standing before a brilliant white temple with your two spirit guardians. It is a very plain, unadorned building with an open doorway. Green trees and bright flowers make a park-like setting around it. Faint notes of a harp are carried on a gentle breeze.

You enter the open doorway and follow a hall toward another door. The walls of this hallway are painted with brightly colored scenes of nature and of the Otherworld. Soon, you see another door, this one closed. One of your guides knocks on the door. A priest of ancient Egypt opens it and glances at you, then at your companions.

"We bring an initiate for cleansing," your guide says.

The priest nods and beckons you all inside. You are standing in a dimly lit room. In the center of the white marble floor is a large circular fire pit, filled with a thick bed of glowing, red-hot coals. A tripod holding a curved basin stands near one side of the pit. A priestess dressed in a long, white robe stands beside it.

The priest leads you to the fire pit and tells you to remove any footwear you might have on. Then he points to the glowing coals, indicating that you must walk across them. You see your guides now standing on the other side of the pit, waiting for you.

"When you reach the center of the fire, stand there for a moment before going on." The priest smiles in encouragement and gives you a pat on the shoulder.

You stand there for a moment, looking at the hot coals, and thinking of what cleansing means. You think of all your negative traits and habits, the old hurtful karmic results in your life—things you need to remove before you can move farther down the spiritual path. You take a deep breath and step out onto the coals.

You immediately realize that there is no burning sensation from the red-hot embers. Also, you cannot walk fast because the coals keep moving under your feet with every step. You must proceed in a slow stroll in order to keep your balance.

When you reach the center of the pit, your feet seem to stick to the coals, not letting you move forward. You understand that you will not be able to proceed from that spot until you release all the negatives in your life to the Element of Fire. One by one, you feel these traits, habits, and karmic results fall away from you. They hit the coals with a loud sizzle and a sudden puff of smoke. This continues until you have released all it is possible to release at this time.

You no longer feel stuck in that spot. You walk on across the hot coals until you reach your guides. They greet you with a smile as they help you step from the fire pit onto the cool marble floor. They lead you around one side of the pit until you reach the priestess standing beside the basin on the tripod. The basin contains what appears to be a mixture of water and liquid fire.

"Be cleansed with this Fire-blessed water," the priestess says to you.

She fills a bowl from the basin and pours the heavy water over your head. As she repeats this, time after time, you see black pieces of remaining negatives flow away with this strange water. You feel lighter and happier now that you have shed so much negative weight.

After the priestess has poured several bowls of the strange water over you, a vaporous cloud forms around your body. Soon, you can no longer see your guides or the priestess. As the cloud gets thicker, you feel yourself moving quickly back to your physical body.

You think of your physical body. You slide down the tunnel of light into that body. You open your eyes. The meditation is finished.

Working With Fire Elementals for Shapeshifting

Sit in a comfortable chair with your hands in your lap and your feet flat on the floor. Make certain you will not be disturbed by the telephone, someone at the door, pets, or any other people in the house. It may be helpful to play a CD of soft nature sounds, to mask any slight background noises. If you put each meditation on a tape, leave spaces in the appropriate places so that you have time to explore or listen to whoever is speaking to you.

Visualize a brilliant white light surrounding and penetrating your body. This is your protection throughout the meditation. Now, slowly begin to relax your body, beginning at the feet and ending at the head. During this time, breathe steadily and evenly. Breathe out all the negatives and troubles in your life. Breathe in the white light of healing and balance.

You are standing in the center of a large room surrounded by rows of metal shelves that reach from floor to ceiling. These shelves are filled with thousands of lighted candles of all shapes and colors. When you look closer, you see that a fire faery dances in each candle flame. The flames flutter and lean from one side to the other from the movements of these beings. Beside you, on a tall stand, is a large candle with several lighted wicks in it. Five faeries are wildly dancing in and out of these candle flames, leaping from flame to flame in a circular dance. However, these particular faeries look at you from time to time, and beckon you to step closer.

As you stand nearer to the candle, one of the faeries stops his wild dance and steps out of the flame. He leaps closer to you and speaks.

"Would you like to go on a shapeshifting journey?" he asks. "You know, shapeshifting is really a state of mind, not a reforming of the body. By accepting the energy of the creature you want to be, your aura becomes full of this energy, and you mentally take on the needed traits and strengths of that creature."

You nod in agreement.

"Come with us," the faery calls to the others on the candle.

Instantly, you are surrounded by a wildly dancing ring of faeries. They spin faster and faster until watching them almost makes you dizzy. As they blur in your vision, you feel yourself moving very fast to another place. When the faeries stop spinning, you are standing at the edge of a large meadow near a thick forest.

"Flying first! Flying first!" chant the faeries.

"Think of a flying creature you would like to be," the male faery says. "Then think how it would feel to be inside the mind and skin of that being."

You decide upon the bird you want to experience. You think of yourself as being within that bird, until suddenly you feel yourself become that creature. You are looking at the world differently. Your hearing is more acute. Your perception of the world around you changes.

You spread your wings and launch yourself into the sky. You revel in the feeling of air under your wings, the ability to maneuver by leaning or tilting your wings, the freedom of moving through the skies unfettered by ties to the earth. You circle the meadow, aware of small animal life on the ground below you.

Then you hear the mind-call of the faeries and return to your place at the edge of the meadow.

Slowly, you slip out of the bird shape you have made and look around.

"Did you learn how to be more observant?" the faery asks. "Did you learn to move over obstacles?"

You talk to the faery about how you felt while being a bird.

"You need to experience more." The faery taps his foot as he thinks. "Yes, being a wolf could prove valuable."

You close your eyes and think of a wolf. Four legs, fur, intelligent eyes, sharp sense of smell, fearless. You open your eyes and see through wolf eyes. The wind carries the odor of the deer in the forest, of a flock of birds in the meadow, of the Fire faeries themselves. You notice that the sky is dark now with a bright, full moon overhead.

You throw back your head, muzzle to the sky, and howl. Your call is answered by other wolves far away. Swiftly, you turn and run through the forest. You continue to run, smelling all the scents in the night air, until you come to a small creek. You stop and lap at the water.

As you drink, the faeries appear around you. You slip away from the wolf image, back to human, and talk to the faeries about being a wolf.

"Change to a minnow next," one of the faeries suggests.

The first light of dawn creeps through the forest, glinting off the water in the small creek. You look down and see several tiny minnows swimming in the water near your feet.

"Experiencing the Water Element is good." The male faery nods his head.

You think about minnows and sliding through the water. Quickly, you find yourself drifting with the other fish, breathing water as if it were air. The faeries standing on the creek bank look huge to you now. You maneuver around water plants by swishing your tail gently. It is peaceful in the water, yet you dart into the plant shadows with the other fish at the sight of any movement on the bank above.

"The small and vulnerable camouflage themselves," you think. "They don't place themselves in dangerous situations."

You think yourself back to your true form and stand among the faeries on the creek bank. You tell them your thoughts about being in a fish form.

"Come, dance with us," the male faery says. He waves his hand at you, and instantly all of you are back in the candlelit room.

You shrink to the size of the Fire faeries, who are now, once more, dancing in the flames of the large candle. You jump from flame to flame in a circular dance, feeling the joy of energy from the Fire Element.

"Spin faster!" one of the faeries calls to you.

You spin faster and faster in the dance. Suddenly, you whirl away from the candle and back into your physical body.

You think of your physical body. You slide down the tunnel of light into that body. You open your eyes. The meditation is finished.

Magickal Uses of Fire Energy

Remember, Fire Elementals can be very dangerous. Read the descriptions of these Elementals carefully. It is safest to work only with the Fire faeries and the tiny firedrakes. However, even those can cause problems if you lose your concentration.

If you need to substitute oils, herbs, incense, or candle colors in any spell, see the Appendix.

Protection Spell

- ✧ two white candles
- ✧ frankincense incense
- ✧ frankincense oil

Timing: any time constant protection is needed.

Spell: The purpose of this spell is to create an invisible energy/protection ball called a Watcher. The Watcher is usually placed in a spot within a house where it can be fed energy every day. It is programmed to send subconscious alarms to the occupants should they be in danger, and to protect the dwelling and those within it.

Rub the oil onto the candles from the wick to the end. They may be rolled in crushed dragon's blood, if you wish. Set a white candle in a holder on each end of your altar. Light the incense.

Hold your hands about 4 inches apart between the candles. Rub your palms vigorously together until you feel them get warm. Cup your hands as if holding a ball. Concentrate on sending psychic energy from each palm and having that energy meet between your hands. Visualize a ball of energy forming there. When the ball feels as if it is growing, move your hands farther apart. Continue to concentrate and mold this energy until you create a ball as large as you can. Balance the ball on your power hand, and hold it between the two lighted candles. Chant:

> *Watcher, made of Light divine,*
> *Protect this house and all of mine.*
> *Be full of life, both night and day.*
> *Keep ill intent far away.*

Place your Watcher on the back corner of a small table, on top of your bedroom dresser, or in another place where you will remember it. Each day, as you go by, pat the Watcher gently, feed it more energy, and say:

> *Grow and protect, Watcher.*

If you drive every day, make another Watcher to place on the dashboard of your vehicle.

Spell for Destruction of Negative Energies

- ✧ a black candle
- ✧ a red candle
- ✧ a small bowl with a teaspoon of salt in it
- ✧ a small cauldron or metal bowl
- ✧ two pieces of red paper just large enough to place under the candle holders
- ✧ a black crayon
- ✧ patchouli incense and oil

Timing: best done during the waning moon, or on the new moon.

Spell: Trace the circular shape of each candle onto a piece of the red construction paper. On the other piece of red paper that will go under the red candle, draw an arrow pointing toward the black candle. Oil the red candle from the wick to the bottom. Put it in a holder on the right side of your altar, with the circle and arrow under it. Be sure the arrow points in the direction of the black candle. Oil the black candle from the bottom to the wick. Place it in a holder on the left side of the altar. Place the paper with just a circle on it under this candle. Clean your hands.

Position the bowl of salt and the cauldron between the two candles, in the center of your altar space.

Hold the palms of your hands toward the red candle. Chant:

> *Draw in positive energy.*
> *This is my will. So shall it be.*

Hold the palms of your hands toward the black candle. Chant:

> *Destroy all negativity.*
> *As I say, so will it be.*

Hold the bowl in both hands and chant:

> *Salt of earth and purity,*
> *Draw all negatives unto thee.*

Walk through every room of your house with the bowl of salt. Circle each room in a clockwise direction as much as you can. Finish by walking around the room in which your altar is positioned. Return to the altar, and set the bowl back in the center.

Hold your left palm toward the black candle, your right toward the red candle. Say:

> *Out with the bad! In with the good!*

Clap your hands together sharply over the center of the altar. Say:

> *This place now is clean and free.*
> *Only goodness comes to me.*

Take the paper from under the black candle, light it in the flame of the black candle, and drop the burning paper into the cauldron. (Be very careful when working with fire, and work outside, if need be.) Say:

Negativity is destroyed.

Take the paper from under the red candle and repeat the ritual, saying:

Positive energy now fills this house and me.

Put out the candles. Save them to be used in only another protection spell. Do NOT use them for any other kind of spell work.

Take the bowl of salt, which now is psychically filled with negative energy, to a sink. Pour the salt down the drain and rinse out the bowl and sink. Dispose of the burned paper when it is cold.

Spell for Change

✦   an orange candle

✦   a small magnet

✦   a small piece of paper on which you write the change you desire

✦   peppermint incense

Timing: best done during a waxing moon, or on a full moon.

Spell: Set the orange candle in the center of your altar. Light the candle and incense. Place the magnet on top of the piece of paper in front of the candle.

Sit and visualize yourself getting the change you desire. Picture it carefully and fully in your mind. Continue this for five minutes. Extinguish the candle. Repeat this until the candle has burned out. Put the paper under your pillow and leave it there for at least a month. Place the magnet on your refrigerator door, so you can use it.

Spell to Gain Confidence

✧   two straight sewing pins with yellow
       heads on them
✧   a small piece of tumbled carnelian

Timing: best done during the waxing moon, or on a full moon.

Spell: Sit in a comfortable place with the two pins and the carnelian easily accessible. Take one pin at a time. Hold the pin by the head in the fingers of one hand, while rubbing the stone up and down the pin with the other hand. While you are doing this, say:

I draw to me only confidence and inner strength.

Repeat the chant nine times on each pin, one time after the other. Each day, wear the pins in an X formation on your clothing.

Powering Fire Amulets and Talismans

You can use charms of the sun, candles, and lanterns to represent the Fire Elementals. Or you can empower real candles and lanterns to be used at your altar. Again, lay them on a crystal cluster overnight to fill them with

Fire energy. Fire talismans will lead you to enlightenment and help with your energy.

Power Animals

To empower these representations of the power animals, hold or touch each one while chanting the proper chant.

O unicorn of truth and light,
Give me the gift of inner sight.
Success and wisdom, bring to me.
And I shall ever grateful be.

Dark bull of strength and power old,
Teach me the magick I must hold,
To repel evil, negativity,
And show the Light for all to see.

Stone Elixirs for Fire Elementals

To attract and work with Fire Elementals, you will need to make elixirs of black onyx, clear quartz crystal, carnelian, and amethyst. The instructions for clear quartz crystal were given on pages 110–111, and see the instructions for making elixirs on pages 58–60. Black onyx will absorb and transform negative energy or thoughts. Carnelian will cause a spell manifestation to appear sooner, and helps with career success, gaining self confidence, and brings good luck. Purple amethyst aids in opening the psychic senses, strengthens communication with your spiritual guides, and opens doors for spiritual growth. Remember to label each bottle.

Hold each jar in both hands and use the chant for the appropriate stone.

Black Onyx

Although onyx comes in other colors, black is the most useful color for magicians. Wearing it in jewelry will make the person less susceptible to negative vibrations. If cut into a slice and polished, it can be used for scrying, like a crystal ball. It helps to recall past lives, balance karmic debts, reduces stress, and destroys negative energies sent by others.

> *Stone of blackness like the night,*
> *Show me the future, dark or bright.*
> *Far lives remember, old debts erased.*
> *All stress released, and problems faced.*

Carnelian

This stone is a deep orange or reddish-orange color. It is a fast-acting stone, valuable for manifestations and career success. It drives away evil, brings good luck, prevents other people from reading your mind, helps with memory, and is very useful in healing the body, especially the blood.

> *As orange as sunset at twilight,*
> *Bring me good luck, successes bright.*
> *Protect the body, soul, and mind*
> *From ill wishes by the evil kind.*

Amethyst

The clear, deep purple amethyst is the color known to most people. It can open gateways for intense, transformational physical or spiritual changes. It can bring any kind of change into your life. It also protects against black magick and promotes spiritual growth.

> *Open the door to changes great,*
> *Transform my life, as is my fate.*
> *Expand my physical life and soul.*
> *Positive changes is my goal.*

Gift to the Fire Elementals

The safest gift to give the Fire Elementals is to burn various types of incense.

Soul Mate Heart, Part 3

Take the red paper heart to your altar and open it to reveal what you wrote about the physical and mental qualities you want in a soul mate. This time, write the spiritual qualities you desire in this person, such as being open minded, nonjudgmental, and other similar traits. When you are finished, refold the paper. Hold it over your own heart and say:

> *Deep love and passion, spiritually,*
> *Are the qualities you must bring to me.*
> *Soul mate strong and lover bold,*
> *Bring me all my heart can hold.*
> *A perfect pair is what we'll be.*
> *So say I. So shall it be.*

THE ELEMENT OF WateR

*Like still Water, be at peace and
balanced in your emotions.*

This Element is wet and in some kind of liquid form. The Welsh use the term *fluidity* to mean moisture or flux.

Many ancient cultures considered Water to be the strongest of all the Elements. The steady drip of water will eventually bore a hole in a stone. In its usual form it uses gentle persistence rather than brute force. Ordinary Water can reshape its circumstances without destruction of what lies in its path. However, in huge amounts, this soft Element is also capable of total destruction.

The tarot suit associated with the Element of Water is cups. This expresses both emotions and love.

To the Norse, the dwarf *Vestri* held up the sky and ruled water. The Celtic Western Wind Castle was gray, for twilight or dusk.

The Mayan Bacab for West was black. In ancient Mexican cultures, the West was yellow and represented Earth.

One Native American tradition was that West was black and was connected with a bear. The Spirit Keeper was *Mudjekeewis*. To the Navajo, this direction was yellow, while to the *Zunis* it was blue.

Enochian and Kabalistic magicians believed that the archangel Raphael guarded the West, while the Hebrews said that the Achor, or behind, was in that direction. The Enochian Castle for this direction was green.

The Hindu Tattwas *Apas* was a silver crescent.

In the Chinese system, the West was white and represented metal and autumn.

Water Element Characteristics

Direction: North (South in the Southern Hemisphere).

Description: liquid matter. In Welsh, *fluidity*, or moisture or flux.

Elemental Spirits: nymphs, undines, merfolk, and faeries who tend water plants.

Color: blue. Scots/Irish, gray.

Archangel: Gabriel.

Ruler of the Element: Niksa or Necksa.

Time: sunset, or 6 p.m. and autumn.

Plane: astral.

Senses: taste.

Property: cold and moist.

Power Animal of Light: salmon, dolphin.

Power Animal of Dark: sow, boar.

Tattwas: *Apas*, a silver crescent.

Tarot Suit: cups.

Kabalistic World: Briah, or the Creative World.

Symbols: lakes, rivers, ocean, wells, springs, pools, rain, mist, and fog.

Astrological Signs: Cancer, Scorpio, Pisces.

Personality Traits: Positive: compassion, peace, forgiveness, and love. Negative: laziness, indifference, instability, and lack of emotional control.

Magickal Tools: chalice, water, mirrors, and cauldron.

Ritual Work: change, divination, love, medicine, plants, healing emotions, intuition, communication with spirit, purification, reprogramming the subconscious mind, pleasure, marriage, sleep and dreams, friendships, and developing the psychic.

The Elemental Spirits of Water

The Elemental Spirits of Water all have strong connections with the earthly version of this Element. Their traditional king is Niksa or Necksa.

Nymphs and undines can be found in small pools and ponds, even waterfalls of any size, while the merfolk, who are their relatives, are found in oceans. Water faeries can be found near the edges of water, such as wetlands, where water plants grow.

The merfolk primarily work with sea creatures. However, all Elemental Spirits of Water work with emotional and mental healing. On occasion, they will cooperate with Elemental Spirits of Earth in manifesting prosperity for humans. These beings are very sensitive but persistent. They will do whatever is necessary to reach a goal.

Traditionally, the Elemental Spirits of Water are the nymphs, undines, merfolk, and a particular type of faery that works with water plants.

Bunyips

These strange water beings are found only in Australia. Although there are different species of the Bunyip type, they live in marshes and swamps all over that country. Bunyips also inhabit dens in river banks, waterholes, and mangrove swamps. They are rarely seen, but stories say that their feet are turned backwards. Their booming roars can be heard over long distances during the rainy season. During a drought, the Bunyips hibernate deep in the mud.

Magickal Uses: Rain.

Kappa

This Water Elemental is found only in Japanese rivers, ponds, and seas. It looks like a furless, child-sized male monkey with a tortoise shell on his back. With skin with a greenish tint, the Kappa has clawed and webbed fingers and toes, with round eyes and a beaked nose. On the crown of his head is a circular depression that holds water; this water enables the Kappa to move about on land. He is surrounded by a constant odor of rotting fish.

The Kappa lies in wait for humans or animals to come near his watery home. He drags his victim into the water and eats it from the inside out. One way to escape the Kappa is to bow to him. When he bows in return, he loses the water in the depression on his head. He has no power until he refills that depression with water.

Although very dangerous, the Kappa will teach the art of bone setting to humans who overcome him by trickery.

Magickal Uses: Not recommended unless the magician has been highly trained in dealing with such beings. In that case, it is used for healing.

Lake Maidens

In Wales, these beautiful Elementals are called the Gwragedd Annwn (gwrageth anoon). They love to sit on the banks of their homes and comb their long golden hair. A member of the Merfolk family, the Lake Maidens sometimes intermarry with humans out of their own free will.

One of the earliest stories of the Lake Maidens comes from the 12th century and concerns the lady of Llyn y Fan Fach, which is a small lake near the Black Mountains in Wales. The story says that a young farm lad fell in love with one of the Gwragedd Annwn. She agreed to marry him if he never showed any violence toward her, not even a love tap. They were happy together for several years, and she bore him three sons. However, the man forgot the promise and gave her three love taps. When he touched her the last time, she returned to her mountain lake.

This lady, though, loved her sons and frequently came to visit them. During these visits, she taught the three boys ancient secrets of medicine. They became the famous physicians of Mydfai. These medical skills descended through the family until the bloodline died out in the 19th century.

Magickal Uses: Healing and medicine.

Lorelei

This Water Elemental is also called the German Mermaid and the Rhine Maiden. The Lorelei became well known to the world in general through the operas of Richard Wagner.

These beautiful young women had fishtails, as mermaids do. They liked to sit on the banks or rocks along the Rhine River, combing their long hair and singing enchanted songs that lured fishermen to their deaths. There is one special rock along the Rhine named for the Lorelei.

These Elemental Spirits are known for guarding magickal treasures. They are also the keepers of ancient knowledge and power that is absorbed into and used by the subconscious human mind.

Magickal Uses: Learning magickal secrets.

Merfolk

Mermaids and mermen are known around the world. They look like humans from head down to the waist; from the waist down they have split fishtails, but no dorsal fins. Usually, their fingers are webbed. Even though the Merfolk are beautiful, it is not a human beauty. Instead, it is emotionless attraction. They can take off their tails to go ashore on two legs.

The Merfolk have underwater homes and frequent the rugged shores of the oceans. They have their own language, but speak many others that they learned during their travels from one place to another. They have strong supernatural powers and the ability to prophecy.

As with the selkies, offspring of one of the Merfolk and a human will have webs between their toes and fingers. However, no mermaid or merman has stayed very long with a human lover.

The Blue Men of the Muir live in the strait between Long Island and the Shiant Islands near Scotland. These are definitely not friendly toward humans. They raise violent storms and throw boulders at passing ships. The only method of handling the Blue Men was to speak in rhyme. Before this branch of Merfolk could interpret the conversation, the human fishermen were gone.

Magickal Uses: Prophecy, inspiration, protection, and developing the psychic.

Nagas

Although the Nagas of India are magickal half serpent and half human creatures, they are also connected with both water and land. The female of this Elemental clan is called a Nagini. Some of the land Nagas are not friendly toward humans. Those that dwell in underwater lairs are adept at using magick and prefer to stay neutral in human affairs.

The water Nagas are the most colorful of their species, and the most curious about humans. If a human presents a sincere petition, you may get their help. They have great powers over all water, and can cause both negative and positive events that have to do with rivers, lakes, ponds, or oceans. Not only can they cause or prevent rain, but they have magickal power over wealth.

Their capital underground city is Bhagavati, which is deep under the Himalayan Mountains. This city is decorated everywhere with rich gems and precious metals. It is also where the Nagas keep ancient books of great magickal knowledge. Every Naga wears a precious jewel on his or her throat or forehead that gives them supernatural powers.

One female Naga is still worshipped today in India. She is the Naga Kanya, or goddess of the three realms. Her upper body is that of a woman, with the lower body of a cobra. The ancient form of the five-headed cobra arches over her head as a sign of her spiritual powers.

She holds a conch shell, symbolizing her willingness to pour out blessings upon humans. She is the guardian mistress of both underwater treasure and spiritual knowledge.

Nagas are guardians of both physical and spiritual treasure. They protect spiritual doors and thresholds and will only allow humans to pass through if the human is worthy and prepared.

Magickal Uses: Seeking the treasure of spiritual knowledge, and understanding where you need to go on your spiritual path.

Nereids

According to the Greeks, the nereids were Water Elementals and the 50 granddaughters of Pontus (a sea god) and Gaea (the Earth Mother). Although they have traits similar to other mermaids, the nereids do not have fishtails. They are very vain about appearance. Frequently, these beautiful nymphs play with the dolphins, riding them through the waves. When Amphitrite, Poseidon's wife, takes out her sea chariot, the nereids surround it.

Magickal Uses: Happiness and balancing emotions.

Nine Daughters of Ran

According to Norse legends, the goddess Ran was one of the wives of the god Aegir. She lived in the seas and used her magick nets to capture the souls of those who drowned or were buried at sea. Ran and Aegir had nine giantess daughters, who also lived in the seas and had unfriendly temperaments like their mother. When Ran created violent storms at sea, her daughters danced wildly on the waves until ships sank and sailors drowned. Then Ran used her magick nets, and her daughters their ghostly white arms, to take the human souls to Aegir's great underwater palace.

Magickal Uses: Not recommended as these Elementals are very unpredictable and malicious.

Nymphs

The Greeks used the name "nymph" to cover certain female Elementals of both water and trees. Actually, even the tree nymphs were connected with water. The Naiads were the nymphs of brooks. The Crenae or Pegae ruled over springs; the Pegae were associated with Pegasus. The more secretive Limnads controlled stagnant waters. The Oreads belonged to grottoes and mountains. The Dryads were of the forests, while the Hamadryads tended certain trees. The Napaeae, the Auloniads, the Hylaeorae, and the Alsaeids were connected with groves and valleys. Often, all of these nymphs chose nearby grottoes, springs, fountains, and pools as their living places.

Magickal Uses: Healing; prophecy; gardening; herbal medicine.

Sea-Lion

This magickal Elemental is not the ordinary creature with which we connect the name "sea lion" today. This is a lion of the sea. It has the mane, head, and foreparts of a lion, but the silvery tail of a great fish. Its forepaws are webbed and clawed. Sea-Lions travel in packs along rocky coastlines, where they hunt fish and sailors. Their roars are so loud they can be heard underwater.

Magickal Uses: Although this is a dangerous Water Elemental, one can work with it for protection from people who play vicious mind games.

Selkies

The people of the Faroe Islands call the Selkies the Seal-Folk. They say that every ninth night, the Selkies come out of the ocean to dance on the beaches. The humans living on the Shetland Islands say that the Selkies only wear their seal skins to get from one place to another, and that they have a human form. They are believed to live in great underwater cities encased in huge bubbles of air. The Shetland and Orkney Selkies, however, will take revenge on seal hunters by raising storms and sinking the ships.

Selkies, male and female, are very beautiful with large liquid eyes. Sometimes, the males will come ashore to court human women, but they never stay with them. The females, like the mermaids, will only stay with a human

man until she finds her seal skin. The people in certain families that trace their lineage back to the union of a Selkie and human frequently have webs between their toes and fingers.

Magickal Uses: Raising storms over water.

Tritons

The Greek race of mermen are called the Tritons and live only in Mediterranean waters. They are human-looking from the waist up but not as handsome as regular mermen; they also have a forked fishtail. Their webbed fingers are tipped with sharp claws. Even the human part of their bodies have tiny silvery scales. Their tangled hair is deep blue or blue-green.

The Tritons do not love human women, but go ashore to drink and lust after the females. They have the ability to remove their tails and walk on two legs on land. Human retaliation through violence is the only deterrent to gangs of drunken Tritons. Their gentle father's name was Triton, and he was the son of Poseidon. His sons, the Tritons, harnessed dolphins to their father's sea-chariot when he journeyed and accompanied him with braying conch shell horns.

Magickal Uses: The Tritons: not recommended. The father, Triton: prophecy, calming emotions.

Undines

The name "undine" comes from the Latin *unda*, which means wave. Because these Water Elementals are not associated with the seas, it is more likely that the word should be "ripples," not "waves." Even the smallest pool of water will have ripples on its surface from wind or ground vibrations.

Undines inhabit every form of water, except the oceans: springs, fountains, creeks, rivers, lakes, fens, marsh, and waterfalls. They range from human size to very small. Although they have scales, as well as webbed feet and hands, the general undine form resembles that of humans. Their appearance reflects their watery surroundings. For example, those of the marshes and fens have stringy, dark hair and fish-like eyes. These are the most unpredictable of the undines, often leading humans astray at night. Some have fishtails, others don't, but they all have webbed fingers and toes. Like the Lorelei, the undines have enchanting voices, however, there is little human about their emotions, personalities, and outlook on life.

Magickal Uses: Controlling emotions.

Water Faeries

Water faeries are some of the smallest of the Small Folk, or one branch of faeries. Their entire life is spent tending to water plants. Their children have fishtails and must stay in water until they mature. As adults, the water faeries resemble tiny humans, the size of dragonflies. In fact, they sometimes ride on dragonflies, either for fun or to journey to another place. The adults can propel themselves up and down waterfalls or in fountain spray. Although they have healing knowledge, the water faeries are unlikely to interact with humans.

Magickal Uses: Healing.

Water Meditation

Meeting Water Elementals

Sit in a comfortable chair with your hands in your lap and your feet flat on the floor. Make certain you will not be disturbed by the telephone, someone at the door, pets, or any other people in the house. It may be helpful to play a CD of soft nature sounds, to mask any slight background noises. If you put each meditation on a tape, leave spaces in the appropriate places so that you have time to explore or listen to whoever is speaking to you.

Visualize a brilliant white light surrounding and penetrating your body. This is your protection throughout the meditation. Now, slowly begin to relax your body, beginning at the feet and ending at the head. During this time, breathe steadily and evenly. Breathe out all the negatives and troubles in your life. Breathe in the white light of healing and balance.

You walk along a smooth, sandy beach at sunset. On each end of this little ocean cove there are rocky cliffs. The ocean is calm. The sound of the waves is soothing. There are thick clouds on the far horizon. You continue to walk along the beach until you reach one of the rock-studded cliffs. A moving patch of pale color catches your eye. You climb over the rocks to see what is hiding in the rock shadows.

As you make your way over the last boulder, you find a tiny section of smooth sand between the rocks. A mermaid is relaxing on that sand, combing out her long bluish-white hair. Her long fishtail floats on the waves, while her human-looking upper body sits on the little beach. Her scales flash iridescent colors in the last light of the sun sinking below the horizon.

She glances at you and beckons with one hand for you to sit beside her. She continues to comb her hair, humming to herself. You make your way through the scattered rocks to sit on the sand near her.

"What do you seek from me, human?" the mermaid finally asks, as she lays aside her shell comb.

"To learn more about communicating with the Elemental Spirits of Water," you tell her.

"You need to remember that emotions, like water, are forever moving and changing," the mermaid says. *"Water Elementals work with the emotions and all things that are in flux in your life. When you learn to still the restlessness within you, you will be better able to communicate with us."*

"Not all Water Elementals are friendly toward humans," you say.

"No. Nor are all human emotions smooth and tranquil," the mermaid answers. *"If you are wise, you learn how to keep a tight rein on negative emotions. As with your life, so with magick. You must keep control and concentration at all times during spell work involving the Elementals."*

You hear a series of booming roars and suddenly see several lion-looking heads break the surface of the water before you. One of these creatures raises a menacing webbed forepaw and smacks the water with its fishtail. The creatures move closer to the shore, watching you constantly.

"The Sea-Lions will not harm you because I am with you." The mermaid tipped her head in greeting to the lion-like creature with its shaggy mane.

"Why is this human in our territory?" You hear the Sea-Lion's words within your mind. The one closest to you appears to be the leader of the pack of Elementals.

"The ocean is not your territory," the mermaid answers. "It belongs to all the sea creatures, humans, and Elementals."

The pack of Sea-Lions turns away, growling deeply. They soon disappear from sight.

"Do not be afraid of them. They are more growl than bite." The voice comes from a seal who pops out of the water. It floats effortlessly in the waves, watching you with large liquid eyes.

"Greetings, Selkie," the mermaid says. "You are late tonight. But then it is your dancing time, isn't it?"

An arm emerges with the water and slides the sealskin off. A man stands up in the water, and walks to your beach with the skin draped over his arm.

"Yes, we have been dancing." The selkie bows slightly to the mermaid. "However, we thought *perhaps your friend here would like to visit one of our underwater cities." Although the selkie now looks very much like a human, you notice it retains its large, dark eyes.*

A second selkie raises its head above the waves to watch you.

"Yes, I would like to visit your city," you say to the selkie as you stand up. "But how will I be able to breathe underwater?"

The second selkie swims closer and holds out a sealskin. You take the skin and step into it. Instantly, the skin molds around your body like your own skin. You join the mermaid and the selkies in the rippling ocean.

Quickly, your companions lead you deep under the water. Before long, you see a bright dome-shape ahead and realize this is one of the bubble-covered selkie cities. Within this transparent dome, you see elegant houses with selkies moving about without their sealskins.

"I will wait for you here," the mermaid says, as the selkies gesture you to follow them through a flexible door into a tunnel.

You go through the flexible, outer transparent door into a short tunnel that leads to another such door. Once inside the second door, you take off the sealskin as do your companions. You leave the skin by the door and look around at the sea-shell decorated houses with meandering paths between them.

Your companions take you on a tour of the underwater city, showing you the schools for the children, the entertainment arena where games and music are played, and the inside of several of the homes. You talk with some of the other selkies and listen to one play a lyre.

As you walk back to the flexible door to the ocean, you see the gang of Sea-Lions swimming around the outside of the protective bubble, their muzzles wrinkled in snarls, their clawed paws raking at the dome. The leader begins to push his way through the outer door into the tunnel.

A conch shell horn is blown in warning by one of the selkies, and the males come running toward the door, armed with sharp, coral-tipped tridents. You see the mermaid flash away toward the surface and safety on the beaches.

"They hunt you," one of the male selkies says. "You must leave at once!"

An older female selkie hobbles up to you and touch your forehead with a twisted, pointed shell that reminds you of a unicorn horn. You feel a burst of power enter your body. Instantly, the selkie city becomes a blur as you slid safely back into your physical body.

You think of your physical body. You slide down the tunnel of light into that body. You open your eyes. The meditation is finished.

Water Faeries and Inland Elementals

Sit in a comfortable chair with your hands in your lap and your feet flat on the floor. Make certain you will not be disturbed by the telephone, someone at the door, pets, or any other people in the house. It may be helpful to play a CD of soft nature sounds, to mask any slight background noises. If you put each meditation on a tape, leave spaces in the appropriate places so that you have time to explore or listen to whoever is speaking to you.

Visualize a brilliant white light surrounding and penetrating your body. This is your protection throughout the meditation. Now, slowly begin to relax your body, beginning at the feet and ending at the head. During this time, breathe steadily and evenly. Breathe out all the negatives and troubles in your life. Breathe in the white light of healing and balance.

You find yourself standing at the edge of a small pond, surrounded by a grove of trees. At the far side, a small stream ends in a waterfall that drops into the pond. The sun is bright on the water, casting shadows from the cattails and other water plants growing at the edges of the pool. Dragonflies hover above the surface, their many different colors bright in the sunlight.

A swarm of what looks like large insects heads toward you. However, you quickly identify them as small water faeries. They are dressed in clothing that blends in with their surroundings.

"Welcome," one of them says. "We have been waiting for you."

The faeries dance in the air in a circle around your head. You glance to one side at a thick growth of cattails. Nearly invisible among the tall stems are several faery houses woven of cattail leaves. Near the water line of these aquatic plants you notice faery children playing with leaves as boats. More faeries are leaping up and down the tiny waterfall on the far side of the pond. The entire pond is full of faery and amphibian life.

As you listen to the faery chatter all around you, you see a nymph slip out of the surrounding trees and slowly lower herself into the water. There is nothing about the nymph to indicate she is not human, except for the green tint to her hair. An undine swims up to her, and they touch hands in greeting. You notice that the undine's hands are very slender and long, with curved nails. She is also long and thin in her body. The two play a game of water tag while you watch from your place among the faeries.

Suddenly, all the inhabitants of the pond grow silent. The nymph climbs out of the water to disappear back into the forest. The undine hides herself among the water plants near the waterfall.

"She is here!" one of the water faeries calls out. "You cannot run from her, human. She is here for you."

"Who is here?" you ask, as the faeries flit away, disappearing in the surrounding foliage.

"The Naga," comes back the soft answer.

Before you can move, a woman's head breaks the surface of the pond. When she is fully visible, you see the upper body of a beautiful woman, but the lower body is that of a great cobra. Her black hair is wound in intricate loops on her head, and a bright jewel decorates the center of her forehead.

Her snake-body is covered with brilliantly colored scales that glow in the sunlight.

"At last we meet," the Naga says as she glides closer to you. You find it impossible to move away from her. "I have come to help you in your spiritual development."

You notice the complete silence hanging over the forest pond. There are no croaking frogs, chattering faeries, or buzzing dragonflies.

Now, the Naga stands directly before you, her hypnotic eyes fastened on yours. You do not feel anything threatening about the Naga. She looks like any woman from India. Yet you are uneasy.

"Why would you help me?" you ask her.

"It is necessary for you to break through old barriers," the Naga answers. "Only in this way can you progress as you should." This time, when she smiles, you see the glistening tips of cobra fangs in her mouth.

Before you can try to move again, the Naga strikes, sinking her fangs into your arm. You feel the poison quickly move through your bloodstream. However, you also note that it does not have a killing effect to it. Instead, you feel your seven chakras cleaning out and balancing properly. Your Third Eye in the center of your forehead, begins to pulsate and open. Your mind is clearer than it has been for some time.

"There is no need to fear," the Naga says as she moves back a step from you. "My bite is much like the elixir of life. There will be psychic changes in your life, and greater spiritual growth than before. This initiation was necessary, or you could not progress."

The Naga smiles and waves her hand gently at you. The Naga and the pond disappear from view. You find yourself sliding back into your physical body.

You think of your physical body. You slide down the tunnel of light into that body. You open your eyes. The meditation is finished.

Magickal Uses of Water Energy

Be certain that your emotions are balanced and in control before working with Water Elementals. They can easily influence your emotional status one way or the other. Their influences are usually subtle, but under unbalanced conditions, their powers can hit the magician like a tidal wave.

If you need to substitute oils, herbs, incense, or candle colors in any of the following spells, see the Appendix.

Calm Emotions Spell

✧   aquamarine or blue topaz
✧   jasmine incense
✧   a mermaid
✧   seashell or anchor charm
✧   a neck chain if you plan to wear
     the charm.

Timing: best done during a waxing moon, or on a full moon.

Spell: Light the incense on your altar. Sit quietly near your altar until you feel calm and in control of your emotions. Run the charm through the incense smoke. Then rub it all over with the stone. Hold the charm in your power hand. Place that hand against your forehead, and say:

Calm as smoothest water deep,
Silent as a mountain lake,
Unruffled as a wind-less night,
My own emotions I will make
As calm as these. For I decree
That as I wish, so will it be.

Either wear the charm on a chain around your neck or carry it in a pocket. You can also carry the stone with you, or wear the stone in a piece of jewelry.

Repeat the cleansing in incense smoke and the chant at each new and full moon for as long as you feel it is necessary.

Breaking Emotional Ties

Sometimes it becomes necessary to break ties with people to whom we are emotionally bound and no longer wish to be.

- ✧ a silver or clear light gray candle to remove negatives
- ✧ a blue candle for the emotions
- ✧ a candle representing your zodiac sign
- ✧ patchouli incense
- ✧ lotus oil
- ✧ a photo of you and the person involved, or a paper with both your names on it
- ✧ pair of scissors
- ✧ a piece of black thread
- ✧ a cauldron

Timing: best during the waning moon, or on a new moon.

Spell: Rub lotus oil on your zodiac candle from the end to the wick; place this candle in the center of the altar. Rub the oil on the blue and silver candles from the wick to the end. Place the silver candle on the left side of your altar, and the blue candle on the right side. Light the patchouli incense. Put the photo or name paper and the candle in front of you, near the center of the altar.

Cut off two 10-inch long of black thread. Tie one end of each thread to the zodiac candle. The other end of one thread is tied to the silver candle, while the remaining thread is tied to the blue candle.

Hold the photo or paper in your hands. Say:

I call a parting twixt me and thee,
These ties can no longer be.
For the good of both, we two must part.
No ties shall be from heart to heart.

Using the scissors, cut the paper between the two names, or the photo between yourself and the other person. Light the pieces from the silver candle, and drop them into the cauldron to burn.

Cut the black thread tied between the candles. Let the candle burn out. Dispose of the wax and remaining thread, if any.

Breaking Negative Karmic Ties

- ✧ a black candle
- ✧ an indigo candle
- ✧ pine incense
- ✧ wisteria oil
- ✧ piece of black onyx
- ✧ a piece of jewelry that holds special significance to you. (If you have black onyx set in a piece of jewelry, this is even better.)

Timing: best done during the waning moon, or on a new moon.

Spell: Rub the oil on both candles from the end to the wick. Place the black and indigo candles in the center of your altar, about 3 inches apart. Light the incense. Hold the black onyx stone and/or jewelry in your power hand. Touch this hand to the side of the black candle and say:

> *I break the bond between us,*
> *No more shall we be tied.*
> *All karmic bonds are broken.*
> *By this word shall you abide.*

Touch your hand to the side of the indigo candle and say:

> *All karmic debts are balanced.*
> *We go our separate ways.*
> *We owe nothing to each other,*
> *From now through future days.*

Run the stone and/or jewelry through the incense smoke. Say:

> *Be you cleansed and powerful.*

If the onyx is set in jewelry, rub the jewelry with your fingers. If the stone is separate, gently rub the jewelry with the stone. Say three times:

> *I build my power from this hour.*
> *No ties remain, to rise again.*

Wear the jewelry every day until you feel that the karmic ties are broken. Repeat the spell each new moon, if necessary.

Calling in Your Astral Animal Helpers

- ✧ four clear crystal points
- ✧ frankincense incense
- ✧ dried sage leaves
- ✧ a large abalone shell

Timing: best done during the waxing moon, or on a full moon.

Spell: Place the abalone shell in the center of your altar with the sage leaves in it. Arrange the four crystal points equal distances around it, points toward the shell. Light the frankincense incense. Light the dried sage leaves and let them smolder in the shell. Run your hands through the sage smoke, and say:

Helpers of old, with powers bold,
come to my call.
My mind calls to you, with desires true.
Come one and all.

Sit quietly for as long as you can, letting your mind flow where it will. Take note of any images that appear in your thoughts. If you see various pictures of the same creature three times, it is revealing itself to you as an animal helper. If you see only one creature, do not be discouraged. Others will reveal themselves later.

Self-Cleansing Ritual

- ✧ candle of your zodiac color
- ✧ cedar or frankincense incense
- ✧ cinnamon oil
- ✧ dried sage leaves
- ✧ a large abalone shell

Timing: best done during a waxing moon, or on a full moon.

Spell: Rub the oil on the candle from the wick to the end. Place the candle in the center of your altar. Put the abalone shell holding the dried sage leaves beside it. Light the incense. Next, light the sage leaves and let them smolder in the shell. Say:

> *By the mighty power of three,*
> *My entire being shall be,*
> *Cleansed to the core and whole,*
> *In my body, mind, and soul.*

Wave the sage smoke toward you with one hand so that it touches as much of your body as possible.

Sit quietly now, and visualize yourself standing beside a deep hole in the ground. Mentally, throw every negative event, feeling, and person into that hole. This can include your own bad habits. Continue to visualize this until your spirit feels lighter.

This spell may be repeated as often as you feel is necessary.

Powering Amulets and Talismans

To empower amulets and talismans of Water Elementals, use the charm symbols or statues of mermaids, seashells, fish, or anchors. Lay these on a crystal cluster overnight to fill them with Water energy.

Power Animals

To empower the representative symbols of these beings, hold or touch each one while chanting the appropriate chant. The dolphin is for light, the boar for dark.

Ocean arrow, rider of waves,
Finder of treasure and under-sea caves,
Steeds of Poseidon, teach me your lore,
Of schools long forgotten, of past times and more.
Open my mind and my heart to your kin,
That I might have knowledge to work with and win.

Creature of power and confidence great,
Help me to face and to break up dark fate.
Teach me the courage to stand and protect,
To turn aside negative, and darkness reject.
Your tusks are your weapons,
your swiftness your shield.
Dark boar of power, teach me not to yield.

Stone Elixirs for Water Elementals

To attract and work with Water Elementals, you will need to make elixirs of agate, bloodstone, blue topaz, hematite, lapis lazuli, seashells, and tigereye. See the instructions for making elixirs on pages 58–60. Remember to label each bottle.

Agate

Blue with white stripes, agate aides in developing the psychic and having visions and meaningful dreams.

Open the doors to visions and dreams,
Make all clear, not as it seems.

Bloodstone

A dark green stone with red flecks, bloodstone guards against deceptions, brings prosperity, tears down walls between you and gaining your desires, and opens you to inner guidance.

Tear down the walls between me and success,
Guide me to truth and happiness.

Blue Topaz

This stone comes in a range of colors, but blue is the most useful. It balances the emotions, heals, helps to commune with spirit guides, and provides inspiration for creativity.

Spirit guides of inspiration,
Come to me with no hesitation.
Balance me in mind and heart,
Remain with me, and do not part.

Hematite

An opaque black or dark iron-gray color with a metallic luster, it increases resistance to stress, gives optimism and courage, and helps to focus on past lives.

> *Old lessons learned within my past,*
> *Will now reveal themselves at last.*
> *From where I've been, to where I go,*
> *Inner knowledge will always flow.*

Lapis lazuli

Deep blue with tiny pieces of gold iron pyrite and off-white patches of calcite, Lapis lazuli releases tension and anxiety, helps with commune with spirit guides, strengthens psychic abilities, and erases karmic debts you no longer owe.

> *Holy stone of mystery,*
> *Bring aid and comfort unto me.*

Seashells

All have a strong connection with the Goddess and the Element of Water. Helps work through emotional issues, find past lives (conch shell), aids in dealing with heavy karma (paua shell), calms nerves and stress (abalone and paua shells), and draws prosperity (clam shells).

> *Strong energies from oceans deep,*
> *Help me my own emotions keep,*
> *Balanced in the spiritual sight,*
> *Of love and goodness, truth and light.*

Tigereye

Golden brown with yellow bands, tigereye balances emotions, grounds and centers, discerns the truth, enhances psychic abilities, and finds karmic ties with others.

> *Like the jungle tiger bold,*
> *Reveal to me the power of old,*
> *That truth and karma I may see.*
> *This is my wish. So shall it be.*

Gift to the Water Elementals

When it rains, or when you are near a stream, river, or the ocean, touch the water with one hand, or catch rain in your hand. Chant:

> *Water Spirits, soft and gentle,*
> *Listen to me, you Elementals.*
> *Your power is welcome in this land,*
> *For love and cleansing go hand in hand.*

Soul Mate Heart, Part 4

Take the red paper heart to your altar. Open it to reveal what you wrote about the qualities you want in a soul mate. This time, add the emotional traits you desire in this person, such as even tempered, gentle, kind, loving, faithful, and other such personality traits. When you are finished, refold the paper. Hold it over your own heart and say:

Soul mate, will you come to me,
And one heart together we shall be.
Joined soul and body, heart and mind,
Great happiness together we will find.

THE ELEMENT OF SpiriT

The Nebulous Realm and Existence of the Element of Spirit

*Like Spirit, be at one with
everything in existence.*

The fifth Element, or the Element of Spirit, is derived from a balance of the other four Elements. It is found in the Center of those Elements. This corresponds to the center of a magickal circle, where the altar is often placed. It is pure ether.

To the Celtic and Norse cultures, the Center or Spirit was represented by the World Tree, or Tree of Life, and white brilliance. Many world cultures used the tree or center pole as Spirit and a means of moving from this world into the Otherworld. Sometimes, the Tree was portrayed as burning, but never consumed. This burning Tree fits with the Welsh description of the South, which detailed it as symbolizing *awen*, or fiery inspiration. This kind of divine inspiration was considered necessary to be a true Bard or spiritual seeker. Using the Tree to represent the center of the mortal world, the Celtic mystics were able to describe the boundaries between the physical world and the Otherworld. Some of the other boundaries that helped to enter the Otherworld were twilight or dawn, and the edges of the sea or lakes. These marked potential gateways through which the mystic could pass from one world to another.

In the Native American Zuni tradition, the Center was a mixture of all colors. The same identification of color was used by ancient Mexican cultures.

The Hindu Tattwas used a black or indigo colored ovoid with pointed ends to represent Akasha, or Spirit and the Center.

One Chinese system believed that the Center symbolized Earth and was yellow.

Spirit Element Characteristics

Direction: the center, or straight up.

Description: Primal Matter. Vital, creating energy that has no form, but balances and blends together all the other Elements. In Welsh, *Nwyvre*, or every life, every soul, and, from its union with other Elements, other living beings. The Druids knew this Element as *nyu*.

Elemental Spirits: angels and archangels.

Color: Traditionally, black and white set together. A blend of all colors, or white brilliance.

Archangel: Metatron.

Ruler of the Element: the God and the Goddess.

Time: time that is "not a time."

Plane: beyond comprehension.

Senses: none.

Property: none.

Power Animal of Light: white dragon.

Power Animal of Dark: black dragon.

Tattwas: ovoid with pointed ends representing Akasha

Tarot Suit: none.

Kabalistic World: Ain, or the Unknowable Spiritual World.

Symbols: the spiral, infinity, the cosmos, deities.

Astrological Signs: none.

Personality Traits: none.

Magickal Tools: the cast magickal circle.

Ritual Work: finding your life path, understanding karmic paths in life, enlightenment, spiritual development, connecting with the Supreme Power behind the deities, and achieving a state of perfect blend of all Elements.

The Elemental Spirits of Spirit

Angels were found in many ancient cultures long before the Christians talked about them. These Elemental Spirits are described in nearly all the religious sacred books. The Egyptians, Romans, Greeks, Persians, Muslims, Japanese Shintoists, Jewish Kabalists, Hindus, and the Maori are among the cultures that believed in angels. Such ancient thinkers as Socrates, Plato,

Paracelsus, Pythagoras, Homer, and Swedenborg all wrote about angels.

The archangels and all other classes of angles are said to be pure radiant energy. They are Elementals of Spirit, and did not evolve along human lines. A powerful, brilliant light comes from the crown of their heads and encircles their entire form, giving the appearance of great wings. They use this field of energy to propel themselves from one place to another.

The word "angel" comes from the Sanskrit word *angiras*, which means a divine spirit or messenger. The Persians called them *angaros*, and the Greeks *angelos*. However, the Greeks also knew them under the name of *daimon*, a supernatural being who mediates between humans and deities. The Hebrews got their idea of angels from the Persians and Babylonians during their captivity.

The term "archangel" symbolizes a pure spiritual being that has progressed to the top of the angelic hosts. Often the names and/or the spelling of these archangels changes from source to source.

In ceremonial magick, five archangels are called upon during ritual. These are Raphael (East), Michael (South), Gabriel (West), Auriel or Uriel (North), and Metatron (center). However, some ceremonial magicians also call upon demons, or fallen angels.

Angelic names have been assigned to the days of the week, the months, and the zodiac. Beyond these, there are archangels and angels who have very specific powers, and can be called upon for help in certain personal areas. Although these Elementals have a human-like form, they are not humans nor have they ever been human. Although these beings are spoken of as "he," they are not male or female.

Archangels and angels are only associated with the Supreme Power, or the God and the Goddess. They are protectors, healers, teachers, and messengers. They hold the keys to the astral doorways that open into other dimensions. Some of these gates open into crossing-time areas, besides the future and the past.

Archangels and Angels

Adnachiel: Angel of November that rules over Sagittarius.

Ambriel: Angel of May that also rules over Gemini.

Asmodel: Angel of April that rules over Taurus. In the Coptic books and the Kabala, this being is called a demon of punishment.

Azrael: Although this angel is not named in the Koran, he is known as the Angel of Death in Islamic writings.

Barakeil: The angel of February with domination over lightning and success in games of chance. He also rules Jupiter and Scorpio.

Barbiel: The angel of October. Tradition says he serves in the Underworld as one of Seven Electors.

Camael: Ruler of Mars, he is called the Avenging Angel. He rules over divine justice, discretion, energy, courage, exorcism, purification, and protection.

Cassiel: A ruler of Saturn, he is the angel of tears and solitude; also of temperance.

Gabriel: One of the two highest archangels. He rules over the moon, the West, and Water. Known as Jibril to the Arabs, he is the angel of visions, magick, astral travel, scrying, herbal medicine, mercy, truth, and hope.

Hamaliel: The angel of August and Virgo.

Haniel: Angel of Venus, December, and Capricorn. He helps to defeat evil. Angel of love, beauty, creativity, and all nature.

Harut and Marut: Two fallen angels mentioned in the Koran. Teachers of magick.

Israfil: Although he is not mentioned in the Koran, this is an Islamic archangel. His sole purpose is to blow the trumpet that will raise the dead at the end of the world.

Jibril: The Arabic version of Gabriel. He revealed the Koran to Mohammad.

Metatron: Known as the Great Teacher, this angel rules the Center, or the Element of Spirit. According to the Kabala, he is the first of the 10 archangels in the Briatic world of the Tree of Life. As the link between humans and the Divine, he rules over spiritual enlightenment and mystical illumination.

Michael: He is considered to be the greatest of all angels and archangels in Christian, Jewish, and Islamic writings. He rules the Element of

Fire, the South, and Mercury. He helps with finding the truth, knowledge, divination, and philosophy.

Muriel: The angel of June and Cancer.

Raphael: This is the angel of the sun; he rules over Air and the East. An angel of healing, harmony, prosperity, success, honor, and contacting your guardian angel.

Ratziel: Called the Prince of the Knowledge of Hidden and Concealed Things, he is the archangel over illumination, guidance, and destiny.

Sammael: Called the Prince of Demons and Magicians, and the Angel of Death, he is spoken of as both good and evil. He rules over death, temptation, punishment, and retribution.

Sandalphon: The twin brother of Metatron and master of heavenly song, this is the angel of prayers, visions of your guardian angel, grounding, guidance, and protection.

Tzadquiel: A ruler of Jupiter and one of the guardians of the East, he rules over spiritual love, inner plane teaching, and good fortune.

Tzaphiel: One of the angels of the moon.

Tzaphkiel: The angel of Saturn who mediates with the forces of karma. He rules over spiritual development, overcoming grief, and changing karma.

Uriel or Auriel: Known as the Archangel of Salvation, he rules the Element of Earth and the North. He is called Israfil in Arabic. He rules over teaching, insight, stability, endurance, and spiritual knowledge.

Verchiel: The angel of July and Leo.

Spirit Meditations

Archangels of the Five Elements

Sit in a comfortable chair with your hands in your lap and your feet flat on the floor. Make certain you will not be disturbed by the telephone, someone at the door, pets, or any other people in the house. It may be helpful to play a CD of soft nature sounds, to mask any slight background noises. If you put each meditation on a tape, leave spaces in the appropriate places so that you have time to explore or listen to whoever is speaking to you.

Visualize a brilliant white light surrounding and penetrating your body. This is your protection throughout the meditation. Now, slowly begin to relax your body, beginning at the feet and ending at the head. During this time, breathe steadily and evenly. Breathe out all the negatives and troubles in your life. Breathe in the white light of healing and balance.

You are standing in the middle of a wide green lawn. You see a tall arch standing a little distance away. The ground around it is rocky and barren, yet you hurry toward it. You stop before the arch to look at it closely. It is made of pale

*granite, sparkling from within with tiny points of
light. Carved deeply into the keystone of the arch
are ancient symbols. As you pass through the
arch, you realize that you are being transported
into another plane of existence. You will be constantly protected and do not need to worry or be
afraid.*

*When your rapid movement stops, you find
yourself in an even more desolate region. It is barren and rocky, with great cracks in the ground
sending out plumes of smoke. The puffs of smoke
are followed by leaping flames. All around you
the flames rise and fall, filling the darkened sky.
You feel the great heated winds that are borne of
the leaping flames. You hear the hiss and crackle
of the subterranean-born fires. Great streaks of
brilliant lightning strike down from the black skies
to mingle their heat and power with the flames
rising from within the ground.*

*You feel compelled to become one with the
Fire Element around you. You merge with the
flames, feel yourself rise and fall as they do. You
feel the tremendous strength for destruction and
creation. You become one with the Fire. As you
experience this oneness with the Element of Fire,
you see standing before you the Archangel Michael.
His eyes are like fiery suns, his white robe brilliant, his upraised sword twined with red flames.*

"I give protection, courage, and help with problem solving," he tells you.

Michael parts the flames with his great sword, and you step out onto the cool shore of a deep mountain lake.

The deep blue-green waters of the lake lap rhythmically and gently against your feet. You feel the lunar pull coming to you through the water. You are drawn to become one with the Element of Water. You slip quickly through the waters of the lake, experiencing the restrained power of this mountain water. You float peacefully and easily until you reach a bubbling, tumbling stream that splashes from the lake off through the mountains toward the sea. You float down the stream, experiencing its happy passage, feeling its strength growing as other little streams merge with it. You feel the controlled power as it smoothes the stones in its gravel bed. You feel the intelligences of the life forms that live in the water, that the stream feeds and protects.

Without warning, you sense a tremendous surge of power. Suddenly, you are part of a great waterfall, crashing, roaring, sending up clouds of spray.

Before long, you feel a greater and greater pull, leading you onward until you merge with an ocean. Once again, you become aware of the many life forms within these deep, dark, rolling, surging waters. You begin to understand the partnership between the great waters and the life within it. You can feel the influence of the moon, creating the oceanic tides and currents, the winds across the surface.

As you flow with the ocean tides, resting within the powerful, yet gentle, arms of the water, you see before you the Archangel Gabriel. His eyes are like deep pools, his blue robe gently ebbing and flowing around him.

"I give you psychic power and visions," he says.

Gabriel raises his hand, and you feel yourself drawn up from the ocean into the great storm clouds hanging overhead.

You have now entered the Element of Air. You are aware of the great strength to create and destroy. You let yourself become one with the storm. You ride with it as it strikes the coastline in its fury—lightning flashing, rain pouring down upon the earth. You continue to feel its power as you go with it up the mountains, lashing the trees and craggy peaks. You notice when the rain turns into soft, cold snow that frosts the mountaintops.

As the storm dips down the other side, the winds drop into a gentle breeze. You ride this breeze as it crosses a desert, stirring the whispering sand. You flow with it as it rushes to caress a woodland, gently stirring the tree branches. The songs of birds fill the air as they happily rise through the air currents. You are aware of the loving caress that the breeze gives to all things that it touches.

As if from nowhere, you suddenly see before you the form of the Archangel Raphael. His pale yellow robe billows about his form of light. His hair crackles and moves about his head in response to every breath of air.

"I give the power of healing," he tells you.

He touches you gently. You feel the power for healing yourself and others flow into you. You drift down until you touch and merge with the Element of Earth.

You let yourself sink deep into the rich soil of the forest floor. You feel the questing roots of plant life as they seek food and water within the earth. You can hear, sense, and see the many forms of insect and animal life that inhabit the darkness of the soil.

You change the direction of your awareness. You then become one with the shifting sands of the desert, experiencing the inhabitants of this different part of earth. You feel the coolness of the oasis water and the little breezes that play across the surface of the desert.

Your awareness shifts again, and you become one with the soil of a jungle floor. You can feel the steamy richness that comes from the decaying tropical foliage. You see and sense the abundance of life within the dense jungle.

As you continue to experience this oneness with the Element of Earth, you begin to feel the heartbeat of the planet. You notice that the Archangel Auriel is now beside you. His rich green robe gives off a scent of flowers and growing things.

"I give you insight and stability," he tells you. "I teach all things."

As you gaze into his golden eyes that are the color and intensity of the sun, you are lifted into the Element of Spirit.

The Archangel Metatron awaits you. He is clothed in dazzling white, his body luminous with spiritual energy. The two of you stand on the rocky floor of a great cavern. The smooth stone walls are translucent white with veins of pastel colors.

Metatron points to a series of naturally-formed steps in the living rock. The stairs lead upward into a shaft of light.

"I give spiritual development and mystical illumination," he says. "An ancient sacred place lies at the top of the stairs. You must go there."

You climb the steps into the light. At the top is an open doorway between two great stone pillars, one black and one white. You pass between the columns into the very center of a temple. The black lustrous floor reflects the ethereal splendor shining from the walls. The walls themselves are of translucent gemstones, molded one into another to produce a multicolored surface.

At the far end of the room is a great silvery curtain embroidered with the staff of Hermes— the staff that is entwined with twin serpents. The curtain shimmers and gently moves with a life of its own. Before it, stands a smoking incense bowl. The perfume of the incense wafts throughout the temple. Above, suspended from the high ceiling, hangs a brilliant silver light, so brilliant that it appears as if a star has been plucked from the heavens and hung in this place.

A stone bench with a deep blue cushion sits beside the censor and before the silver curtain. The absolute calm of the temple enters you, filling you with an understanding of the balance and perfection of the universe.

You sit on the bench, awaiting guidance from the Element of Spirit. You hear faint messages come into your mind, and you will remember them. As the inner voice stops speaking, a breeze blows the incense smoke onto your face. You feel your-self sliding back into your physical body.

You think of your physical body. You slide down the tunnel of light into that body. You open your eyes. The meditation is finished.

Meeting the Angels

Sit in a comfortable chair with your hands in your lap and your feet flat on the floor. Make cer-tain you will not be disturbed by the telephone, someone at the door, pets, or any other people in the house. It may be helpful to play a CD of soft nature sounds, to mask any slight background noises. If you put each meditation on a tape, leave spaces in the appropriate places so that you have time to explore or listen to whoever is speaking to you.

Visualize a brilliant white light surrounding and penetrating your body. This is your protection throughout the meditation. Now, slowly begin to relax your body, beginning at the feet and ending at the head. During this time, breathe steadily and evenly. Breathe out all the negatives and troubles in your life. Breathe in the white light of healing and balance.

You are standing in a beautiful garden. Around you are trees and flowers of all colors and kinds. You see several paths leading off through the garden. You chose one and follow it through the beauty of nature.

The Ancient Ones used to talk to the spirit of the trees, the flowers, the running water. Take time now to feel the brotherhood you share with every animate and inanimate creation. Even rocks and minerals are alive with the Element of Spirit. Each wayside stone is vibrating with a light and life it shares with every other thing in creation.

Your vision is becoming clearer. You see all the flowers and trees pulsating, vibrating with color and life. All in nature is pulsating with divine fire. You can see this spiritual fire as vibrating tiny sparks of light within everything, even inanimate objects.

Look at a tree. You will see more than its trunk, limbs, and foliage. You can see the divine spiritual fire coming from the earth up into the trees. The fire rises up through the trunk of the tree to radiate light through all its branches and leaves. Spiritual fire is shining not only in the sky, in the rays of the sun, but in the earth itself, and in all nature.

Look up into the heavens. You can see brilliant colored rays streaming down from the planets to the earth. Feel the rays entering your body, healing and strengthening every part. Feel yourself vibrating in tune with all life.

You walk out from under the shady trees and into a meadow. The time has changed to early morning, with the sun just coming up. The butterflies are beginning to flutter from flower to flower. The dew is still wet on the grass and hanging in diamond drops in the gossamer cobwebs. You can feel and see the white light of Spirit in everything around you. It is in the air you breathe, in the water, the sky, the wind, and the plants and animals.

You turn and see before you a golden stairway reaching from the meadow up into the heavens. As you start up the stairway, you are instantly transported into the realm of Spirit.

You find yourself standing before a beautiful temple. Crowds of people are going inside, and you go with them. Inside, the altar of light sits in the center of this huge temple. The arch of the temple roof is receiving a golden stream of sunlight. As you watch this glorious beam of light, you see that it is charged with tiny specks of life-energy whirling in space. You recognize these tiny specks as the same life-energy you saw in the plants, animals, and rocks on the earth.

As you gaze up into this golden light, you begin to hear the faint strains of the most beautiful music you have ever heard. This is the music of the spheres, or planets. As you listen, you feel their harmonies sounding in your own heart.

Suddenly, you are surrounded by colors of the most delicate shades. A multitude of beautiful beings move among you and the others in the temple. Each of these beings vibrates a particular color and note of harmony. One of them is a planetary angel closely associated with you in this present life. Your guardian angel is also among this celestial crowd, as are the angels who help you with your creative and psychic talents. You are free to ask them any questions you wish.

Finally, your guardian angel tells you that you must return to the earthly realm. If there is a message for you or someone else, it will be given to you now. Your guardian touches you gently on the forehead. You feel yourself falling back into your physical body.

*You think of your physical body. You slide
down the tunnel of light into that body. You open
your eyes. The meditation is finished.*

Prayers, Incantations, and Their Effect on the Elements and Elementals

It has been proven in several scientific studies that prayers and incantations have an actual physical effect on plants and animals. Because everything in the universe is connected, prayers, chants, and incantations can affect anything, animate or inanimate. These methods are an important part of healing yourself and others, or creating changes in your life. The following are examples for you to use. You may also create your own prayers and chants. They do not have to rhyme. Chants and prayers are part of concentrated spell work, regardless of your religion, or whether you even believe in spells and magick.

Remember to stay away from using these prayers and spells to control or harm others. You will only create negative karmic circumstances for yourself.

Karmic Path Chant

*From life to life, through history,
My path follows karmic destiny.
I chose goodness to fill my heart,
And break the karmic path apart.*

Balance of Elements Chant

Count the Elements fourfold,
Earth, Air, Fire, and Water,
The fifth is Spirit that holds all
Of the universe together.
Four directions of a circle,
With power in the Center,
Creates a time without a time,
A cauldron of primordial matter.
A sacred place between the worlds,
Where magick lives and can create,
All things desired, all wishes filled,
Can change all lives and karmic fate.

Calling the Angels Chant

Holy beings of high vibration,
I sent to you an invitation.
I need your wisdom and your power,
To guide me in this troubled hour.

Enlightenment Chant

I ask for enlightenment, wisdom old,
To reveal my path, my future unfold.
I turn from dark into the light.
I change from mundane to holy sight.

Powering Amulets and Talismans

You can use charms of a spiral and those representing the Goddess and the God for the Element of Spirit. Lay these images on a crystal cluster overnight to empower them with Spirit energy. Symbols representing Spirit can open inner doors and expand your spiritual path.

Power Animals

To empower the representations of the power animals, hold or touch each one while chanting the proper chant.

White Dragon

Dragon of light, powerful and great,
Keeper of secrets and humanity's fate,
Teach to me the sacred key,
That opens door to infinity.

Black Dragon

Dragon of dark, you balance of power,
Reveal to me your ancient wisdom.
Help me in perfect balance to be,
In all the future days to come.

Stone Elixirs for Spirit Elementals

To attract and work with Spirit Elementals, you will need to make elixirs of emerald, ruby, and sapphire. See the instructions for making elixirs in Chapter 1. Emerald can attract love and new beginnings. Ruby is a stone that represents passionate love. Sapphire is good for breaking up old blockages. Remember to label each bottle.

Hold the jar in both hands and use the chant for the appropriate stone.

Emerald

Shades of green, this stone can charge other stones. It aligns all the bodies, strengthens spiritual insight, enhances dreams, new beginnings, and attracts love and prosperity.

The green of growth and new beginning,
The tint of insight and of dreaming,
Align all life to be its best,
And filled with love and happiness.

Ruby

Usually in true shades of red, but can be pinkish, purplish, or vermilion, ruby protects and stabilizes; removes limitations; aids intuitive thinking; attracts passionate love.

Oh stone of protection and of love,
Reflect those powers from above.
Imbue this water with your power,
And charge it in this moonlit hour,
With all needed energy.
This I do say. So shall it be.

Sapphire

Varying from cornflower blue to deep midnight blue, sapphire breaks up confusion, commune with the Higher Self, intensifies spells, dissolves poverty, and breaks up old blockages.

> *Clear my path, that I might see,*
> *The best and perfect way for me.*
> *Help me dissolve all blocks I find,*
> *Within the body, soul, and mind.*

Soul Mate Heart, Part 5

Take the red paper heart to your altar for the last time. Open it to reveal what you wrote about the qualities you desire in a soul mate. This time add the karmic traits you desire. Take great care in including karma, for you may be paired with a person to work out a karmic debt that is negative. You want to concentrate on good karma, such as happy past lives together or positive karmic compatibility. When finished, refold the paper. Hold it over your own heart and say:

> *I send a call into time and space,*
> *To bring to me my soul mate dear.*
> *Oh angels of the highest power,*
> *Join the two of us together here.*

Put this soul mate heart in a safe place. Each full moon, hold it to your heart and say:

> *I await you, my perfect soul mate.*

Other Interactions

Elemental Energies for Spells

Often, it becomes necessary to combine two or more Elements in a spell so that the spell is more inclusive, stronger, or fast acting. This must be done with great care and much thought about the outcome. Combining Elements is not work for apprentices. The magician should have much experience before venturing into this area of weaving Elemental Magick. Some Elements and Elemental Spirits are not compatible, and will only work together if the opposing Element is added in tiny amounts. For example, Fire and Water really are not compatible. However, sometimes Water needs to be energized or heated. Other times, it needs the emotions evaporated out of it. All magickal spells are formulated according to the desired result.

The following list is one of mere suggestion as to how Elements could be combined and what the results might be. I have kept it simple by showing which spells work best with the combination of just two Elements. The advanced magician may want to experiment with three, or as many as four, Elements in varying amounts or degrees. Before doing this, however, make certain you have a solid working knowledge of the Elements and their Elemental Spirits.

Use more of the first Element listed, and lesser amounts of the second Element listed. This can be accomplished by calling upon several appropriate Elemental Spirits of the first Element, and fewer of the second Element. If, at any time, you feel you need extra control and support, add an Elemental Spirit from the Element of Spirit to your spell.

Earth-Air: Gnomes and dwarves, with sylphs. Inspiration and ideas for a project or job; applying for a job; practical decisions on life issues.

Earth-Fire: Dwarves and elves, with firedrakes. Passionate love, grounded energy for a difficult project, and court visits and lawsuits where you are innocent.

Earth-Water: A difficult combination: Water can wash away Earth, and Earth can hold back Water. Faeries and trolls, with lake maidens. Self-removal from an emotional entanglement, protection from energy vampires, and preparing for tests in classes.

Earth-Earth: Difficult to control: there is a risk of things becoming too rigid, or an overbalance that causes destructive movement. Fox spirits and kobolds. Healing nervous conditions, creating stability in unstable events, and gaining a physical or material desire.

Air-Fire: A difficult combination: Air can intensify Fire and make it uncontrollable. Sylphs and jinns, with salamanders. Gaining desired changes in life, building communication in a relationship, and getting a wish granted.

Air-Water: Pegasus and the winged serpent, with selkies. Learning divination, inspiration for rituals and spell work, and using mental strength to work out emotional troubles.

Air-Earth: Griffin and gargoyle, with brownies. Healing of the physical body; researching past lives, and creating new beginnings.

Air-Air: Difficult to control: air out of control can become storms. Sleipnir and the white eagle of Zeus. Prophecy, learning to trance, and travel in the Otherworld.

Fire-Water: A very difficult combination: each can destroy the other. Salamanders and firedrakes, with the sea-lion. Protection from psychic attack, protection from human enemies, and meeting your astral guides.

Fire-Earth: Alsvidr and Arvakr, with the Old Lady of the Elder. Finding a new life path, learning the proper use of ritual tools, and studying psychic powers.

Fire-Air: A difficult combination: Air feeds Fire. Fire faeries and thunderbirds, with Garuda. Building an energy shield, shapeshifting, and returning ill wishing to the sender.

Fire-Fire: Difficult to control. Vivasvat and Fire faeries. Scrying with a crystal ball or mirror, breaking up illusions, and discovering the truth.

Water-Earth: A difficult combination: Water can wash away Earth, or make it unstable. Water faeries and nymphs, with dwarves. Herbal medicine, healing with stones, and making magickal potions and elixirs.

Water-Air: Lorelei and undines, with Air faeries. Learning a new skill or job, changing professions, and making yourself a love magnet.

Water-Fire: A very difficult combination: each can destroy the other. The archangels Michael and Gabriel. Finding love, visions, and astral travel.

Water-Water: Difficult to control. Merfolk and the Nagas. Seeking ancient spiritual knowledge and strength to follow one's own spiritual path.

Ritual Use of the Elements and Elementals

The more you practice and advance with magick and spell work, the more need you have to learn properly how to cast and close a magickal circle. Magick itself is not a part of any religion. It is a separate practice that can be combined with a religion. To safely and properly work powerful magick, one must do this within the circle.

If the magician works within a consecrated circle, which must be done if attempting certain types of magick, she or he uses the Elements and Elementals in some form or another. This is accomplished by calling up the four directions in the beginning, and bidding them farewell at the end of the ritual.

The magician will also have representations of the four Elements on her or his altar: Candles symbolize Fire, incense is for Air, Blessed salt represents Earth, and the cup of water is naturally for Water.

When working with some of the Elemental Spirits listed in this book, it is safer to learn to cast a circle before calling upon them. Although one should not try to call an Elemental Spirit into actual physical existence, you will be working with the energy of such Elementals. Doing this within a cast circle (with appropriate calling and dismissal of the Elementals) will keep uncontrolled, erratic energy from bouncing around your home when the ritual is finished. "Renegade" magick can quickly create havoc.

A properly cast circle becomes a time that is not time, and a place that is not an earthly place. The magician has literally created a sacred spot that exists on the boundaries between this world and the Otherworld. Thus, the magician is able to form the desired result in the astral energies and will it to manifest into the physical plane of existence. Any magick can be performed without casting a circle, and the smaller magicks often are. However, working within a consecrated circle exposes the magician to accessibility to more energy, and the probability of the spell manifesting much more quickly.

On the following pages, there are a variety of ways to cast a circle and call upon the Elements and Elementals. Try working with several before you choose one that appeals to you. None of them are better than any other; they are all simply methods of wording to produce a desired result.

Although some writers insist that a circle cannot be smaller than 9 feet in diameter, sometimes this size is not practical. The area a magician may have available to work in might be very small. Casting a smaller circle is permissible, as long as the magician has room to move about a little. Obviously, a circle that is barely wide enough to stand in will not be enough space. Nor is an entire room required, although dedicating a whole room to ritual and magick is very nice. A separate room means the magician can leave her or his tools and supplies in place, and merely close the door to keep out unwanted visitors.

To cast a circle, have your altar set in the center with all the tools you need on it. You will need a small cup of water, a plate with a little salt on it, incense, an athame or a wand, one or two white altar candles, and all the ingredients needed for whatever spell you will be working. The spell work is done after the circle-casting. The candles and incense are lit before you cast the circle. Set four candles, one at each of the directions, near the edge of the circle area. Use yellow for East, red for South, blue for West, and dark green for North. The white altar candles represent Spirit, in the center.

Some practitioners prefer the altar set in the East instead of in the center. I prefer a centrally placed altar so I can easily move around it if necessary.

Traditionally, the circle is cast using a sword, however, many magicians find a sword financially out of reach. An athame (dagger), wand, or the forefinger of your power hand (the hand you write with) can be used instead of a sword.

Beginning in the East, and moving clockwise in a circular movement, trace in the air the boundary line of your magickal circle. Visualize this line as blue flames that rise up with your passing. You end again in the East and overlap the ends of the boundary line.

Stand before your altar, with your power hand over the cup of water. Say:

Be fresh and pure in the name of positive power.

Now hold your hand over the plate of salt, and say:

Be cleansed and purified in the name of positive power.

Mix a pinch of salt in the water by swirling the cup at least three times, clockwise. Using the fingers of your power hand, lightly sprinkle the water around the edges of the circle. Begin and end in the East. While sprinkling, say:

> *This sacred place is cleansed and safe*
> *from all negative power.*

Carry burning incense around the edge of the circle while saying:

> *Open the door between the worlds.*

The magician now calls up the four Elements and/ or Elemental Spirits at the four cardinal direction points. Several different examples follow. Choose the one with which you are most comfortable or that fits your needs best.

When calling each Element, stand in that direction in the circle with your hand or athame up in a gesture of salute.

Calling the Four Elements

Lords and Ladies

Go to the East and salute:

> *Welcome, Lords and Ladies of the East. I call*
> *upon you to guard this circle.*

Go to the South and salute:

> *Welcome, Lords and Ladies of the South. I call upon*
> *you to guard this circle.*

Go to the West and salute:

> *Welcome, Lords and Ladies of the West. I call upon you to guard this circle.*

Go to the North and salute:

> *Welcome, Lords and Ladies of the North. I call upon you to guard this circle.*

Archangels

Go to the East and salute:

> *I call upon you, Raphael, to protect me and this circle.*

Go the South and salute:

> *I call upon you, Michael, to protect me and this circle.*

Go to the West and salute:

> *I call upon you, Gabriel, to protect me and this circle.*

Go to the North and salute:

> *I call upon you, Auriel, to protect me and this circle.*

Elemental Kings

Go to the East and salute:

> *Paralda, king of the East and Air,*
> *I ask you bless this circle fair.*

Go to the South and salute:

> *Jinn, king of the South and Fire,*
> *I ask you help create my desire.*

Go to the West and salute:

> *Niksa, king of Water and the West,*
> *guide my hand to what is best.*

Go to the North and salute:

> *Ghom, king of the Earth and North,*
> *bring positive energy forth.*

Elemental Spirits

Go to the East and salute:

> *Sylphs and zephyrs, Elementals of the East,*
> *come join my circle in this place.*

Go to the South and salute:

> *Salamanders and firedrakes of the South, come*
> *join my circle in this place.*

Go to the West and salute:

> *Nymphs and undines of the West,*
> *come join my circle in this place.*

Go to the North and salute:

> *Gnomes and dwarves of the North,*
> *come join my circle in this place.*

Animal Helpers

Go to the East and salute:

> *Eagles, hawks, and falcons, be thou here.*

Go to the South and salute:

> *All reptiles and amphibians, be thou here.*

Go to the West and salute:

> *Dolphins and whales, be thou here.*

Go to the North and salute:

> *Wolves, all land creatures, be thou here.*

Now is the time to do meditation, or any spell work or magick. When you are finished, and before you close the circle, lay your hands on the altar to ground and center yourself once more.

Using your athame or wand, go to each direction and dismiss the Elementals. Begin in the East.

Dismissing the Four Directions
Lords and Ladies

Go to the East and salute:

> *Lords and Ladies of the East,*
> *depart in love and friendship.*

Go to the South and salute:

> *Lords and Ladies of the South,*
> *depart in love and friendship.*

Go to the West and salute:

> *Lords and Ladies of the West,*
> *depart in love and friendship.*

Go to the North and salute:

> *Lords and Ladies of the North,*
> *depart in love and friendship.*

Archangels

Go to the East and salute:

> *My thanks, Raphael, for your aid and power.*

Go to the South and salute:

> *My thanks, Michael, for your aid and power.*

Go to the West and salute:

> *My thanks, Gabriel, for your aid and power.*

Go to the North and salute:

> *My thanks, Auriel, for your aid and power.*

Elemental Kings

Go to the East and salute:

> *Farewell, Paralda, king of the East and Air.*

Go to the South and salute:

> *Farewell, Jinn, king of the South and Fire.*

Go to the West and salute:

> *Farewell, Niksa, king of the West and Water.*

Go to the North and salute:

> *Farewall, Ghom, king of the North and Earth.*

Elemental Spirits

Go to the East and salute:

> *I bid you leave in peace,*
> *sylphs and zephyrs,*
> *all Elementals of Air.*

Go to the South and salute:

> *I bid you leave in peace,*
> *salamanders and firedrakes,*
> *all Elementals of Fire.*

Go to the West and salute:

> *I bid you leave in peace,*

> nymphs and undines,
> all Elementals of Water.

Go to the North and salute:

> I bid you leave in peace,
> gnomes and dwarves,
> all Elementals of Earth.

Animal Helpers

Go to the East and salute:

> Go with my blessing,
> eagles, hawks, and falcons.

Go to the South and salute:

> Go with my blessing,
> all reptiles and amphibians.

Go to the West and salute:

> Go with my blessings,
> dolphins and whales.

Go to the North and salute:

> Go with my blessings,
> all wolves and land creatures.

When you ritually close the circle, you release the spell energy and magick to manifest in physical form. By doing this, you also avoid any uncontrolled power from bouncing around your living space and causing problems.

Closing the Circle

Go to the East and, using your athame or wand, "cut" through the air counterclockwise on the edge of the circle. Say:

> *This ritual is ended,*
> *but the sacred circle remains*
> *invisible and intact.*
> *I leave this place*
> *between the worlds,*
> *but it exists forever.*

Effect of the Seasons and the Moon on the Elementals

Moon phases and earthly seasons affect humans in a variety of ways. Because everything in the universe is composed of the building blocks called Elements, it stands to reason that such powerful changes as moon phases, the Solstices, and the Equinoxes would have an effect on the Elemental Spirits. Some of these effects are listed here.

New Moon

During the waning and new moon phases, the Elemental Spirits most affected are Air and Fire. The pull of the moon's forces is weaker during these times, allowing Air and Fire to have a stronger influence.

Full Moon

Elementals of Water and Earth feel the pull and power of the full moon most. They are stronger during the waxing and full moon cycles than at any other moon phase.

The effective period of each Equinox and Solstice runs from halfway between the last date and the upcoming one, until halfway to the next seasonal date. These in-between periods are considered holy days in Wicca and other Pagan groups. So the powers and effects of each Equinox or Solstice briefly combine with the one behind and the one ahead. These periods between the seasonal passages are the most flexible for magickal use.

Imbolc (February 2)

Earth and Air Elementals affect each other and draw energy from each other at this time. Energy currents within the planet renew themselves and begin life cycles anew. This causes the Air Elementals to change their seasonal patterns and warm to bring forth new life.

Spring Equinox

The Elementals of Air are more powerful and active during this Equinox. These Elemental Spirits also tap into the Water Elementals to produce changes and new growth cycles.

Beltane (May 1)

Here, the Elementals of Air and Fire meet and begin to combine. Sometimes, there is a competition as to who wields the most power.

Summer Solstice

This is the season of the Fire Elementals. Their strong influence is felt in the heat of the summer. Except for violent forms of the Air Elementals, the Fire Elementals are too strong to be overcome by them. Fire is least likely to share space with other Elementals.

Lunasa (August 1)

At this time of year, the battle for power begins between the Fire and Water Elementals. Still, the Fire Elementals are strongest.

Autumn Equinox

The Water Elementals take precedence now, holding back the heat of Fire and the cold of Earth for a time.

Samhain or Halloween (October 31-November 1)

There is a definite mix of Water and Earth Elementals abroad during this time of year. Frequently, Air Elementals will be pulled into the mix, and heavy storms are created.

Winter Solstice

This is the weakest part of the year for Fire Elementals, but the strongest for those of the Earth. The solidness and stability of the Earth Elementals nearly smothers out the others, until the energy tide begins to turn again at the next Imbolc.

Crop Circles and the Elementals

Crop circles have become an exciting subject of discussion in many areas. Their strange overnight appearances, especially in England, have baffled many, as have their complex, geometric designs.

Crop circles, however, are not a new phenomena. The first records of them were written down in the 17th century. If they existed before these records, we do not know. The circles have occurred in various spots around the world, in no discernable pattern of placement. In the beginning, and up until the mid-1980s, they appeared as simple designs: circles, variations of the Celtic cross, or circles with rings. After 1990, the crop circles grew in size and complexity. Some have measured as large as

200,000 square feet. Some of the designs resemble ideas of quantum physics.

Eyewitnesses reveal that some are created before their eyes in under 20 seconds, without the appearance of anything or anyone to make them. The only unusual, and unexplainable, activity is the rare appearance of shafts of light coming from an unknown source in the sky or rapidly moving incandescent balls of light that appear and disappear suddenly.

The continuing complexity of the designs seems to be a symbolic code, sent as a message of many parts for humans to decode and understand. There are symbols similar or identical to those found in many ancient cultures and languages. Others look like strange combinations of quantum physics and science fiction.

There are various explanations put forth by humans and governments as to the creation of crop circles. Some governments would prefer we all ignore them. Humans are divided between creation by space aliens or naturally produced phenomena by the energies within the earth. Another group adheres to the explanation that the circles are made by humans, particularly Doug and Dave of Hampshire, England. This isn't possible because the crop circles appeared before these two men were born, and are still appearing in places where the two men have never been. And the plants within the design are not destroyed as they would be if created with a garden roller or planks. Personally,

I think that the Elemental Spirits, acting under the influence of the Center, or Spirit, are sending important messages to humans. It is up to us to decode the language. Unfortunately, we have no Rosetta Stone language software to help us.

In authentic crop circles, the plant stems are bent, not broken. The plants seem to have been subjected to an intense burst of heat. This causes the area to give off steam, which has been noted by people who quickly find these designs. Three or four hours after the phenomena appears, the soil itself undergoes changes to its crystalline structure, and the ground looks as if it has been baked. These circles are usually formed at night, between 2 and 4 a.m.

All the scientific aspects noted of a crop circle can be coordinated with the four Elements and the Elemental Spirits that exhibit their powers to humans: The pressure of Air bends the plants; Fire creates the brilliant balls of light and the intense heat that blackens part of the stems and bakes the soil; Water is evident in both the plants and steam of such a circle; the energies of Earth may dictate where these circles appear; and they are all controlled by the Elementals of Spirit.

There is also a diversity of opinions as to what this strange coded language is to impart to humanity. Some believe the circles are messages from aliens who are trying to communicate with us. Others, of the doom-and-gloom nature, see them as warnings to clean up pollution or die. Another group, myself included, see these beautiful designs as a method of communication between the Elementals of all the Elements and the humans inhabiting this planet. They may be part warning, part instruction of ancient, forgotten knowledge. Until we manage to decode the symbols properly, we can't be certain.

The frequency and diversity of crop circles should not be ignored, however. Perhaps, if those of us who work with the four Elements, and the Elemental Spirits attached to them, take on the study of crop circles, we will stumble across the interpretation. This could open new doors to learning and knowledge in all areas of human endeavors.

This planet Earth is our home. We are composed of the same four Elements that make up the planet. We interact daily, consciously or not, with the Elemental Spirits belonging to those Elements. We should look upon the Elemental Spirits as another, yet different, level of intelligence, and make a determined effort to communicate more with them. This is an exciting path to consider, a path that can lead us to new ways of interacting with all in the universe. If we learn to establish a communication and more direct connection with the Elemental Spirits, we will be able to conquer any challenges that come our way, even the perfecting of ourselves.

Appendix

Correspondences for Elemental Magick

The following lists can be used for spells and rituals for any of the Elementals, regardless of their Element.

Basic Colors for Magick

Black: This color aids in the absorption and removal of negative energies, brings protection, helps with breakage of blocks, helps repel black magick and negative thought forms, aids in binding negative situations or people. Be careful how you use the color black, as there can be backlash if you aren't skilled in the use of magick.

Blue, Light: Light blue is for inspiration, finding the truth, good health, happiness, inner peace, harmony in the home, learning patience, and communicating with your Higher Self.

Blue, Royal: Royal blue inspires loyalty, brings success for a group, and helps in expanding occult power.

Brown: Especially good for contacting the Earth

Elementals, this color will attract money, financial success, and influence from these Elementals. Brown also helps with concentration, intuition, earthly psychic development, and is grounding and centering.

Gold, very light yellow: Particularly good for gaining fast luck when things are out of your control. Gold and very light yellow attract divination abilities, higher influences, knowledge, wealth, and happiness, and are connected with male deities.

Green: Excellent for contacting nature Elementals, green can help balance an unstable situation. It is helpful in attracting abundance, fertility, material gain, prosperity, success, renewal, marriage, and healing.

Indigo: This very dark purplish-blue Saturn color is so powerful it can neutralize magick sent by another person. Use it to balance karma, stop gossip and lies, block another's actions, or sweep away competition.

Magenta: This color has such a high vibrational rate that it makes spells happen fast. Thus, a candle of this color can be burned along with other candles to hasten results. This cranberry color is a very dark-but-clear red. When burned alone, it is good for quick changes, spiritual healing, and exorcisms.

Orange: Be sure you want major changes in your life, for this vibrant color is very powerful. Orange helps with encouragement and sudden changes, it stimulates energy and creativity, prosperity, mental energy, and enthusiasm. It also changes your luck and brings success.

Pink: This color is for the purest form of true love, friendship, romance, spiritual awakening, and healing. Pink can be used to banish hatred, negativity, or depression.

Purple: This color is so powerful, the energy can be difficult to handle, so use it with care. It helps with success, higher psychic abilities, wisdom, spirit contact, breaking bad luck, divination, strengthening magickal powers, protection, removing hexes and getting rid of bad luck, success in court cases, and influencing people who have power over you.

Red: This color is used for energy, strength, physical desire, passionate love, willpower, good health, conquering fear, and protection against psychic attacks.

Silver, very clear light gray: Associated with the goddess, these colors can neutralize any situation and help in developing psychic powers, aid stability, meditation, and removing negatives.

White: It is a balanced spiritual color, also used for purity, truth, wholeness, to raise vibrations, to raise spiritual awareness, to attain higher goals in life, and to destroy negative energies. Always use white candles when in doubt about what color you need.

Yellow: This color stimulates the intellect, creativity, confidence, concentration, inspiration, mental clarity, business sense, and helps with counseling and healing.

Zodiac Colors

Sometimes in candle-burning spells, it helps to have a candle representing you, along with the others. The following list may vary from author to author.

Aries: red, white, or pink.

Taurus: green, pink, red, or yellow.

Gemini: yellow, silver, green, red, or blue.

Cancer: white, green, or brown.

Leo: gold, orange, red, or green.

Virgo: gray, yellow, gold, or black.

Libra: royal blue, light brown, or black.

Scorpio: black, red, or brown.

Sagittarius: dark blue, purple, gold, or red.

Capricorn: red, black, or dark brown.

Aquarius: light blue, dark blue, or green.

Pisces: aquamarine, royal blue, white, or green.

Incense

It does not matter if you use incense in powdered form, cones, or sticks. Some of the following scents may be difficult to find in cones or sticks. You can make your own incense powder to be burned on religious charcoal (a specialty) by mixing appropriate herbs with a base of sandalwood powder and a few drops of oils. You can use lotus, frankincense, or a mixture of frankincense and myrrh for any ritual or spell.

Balance: jasmine, orange, or rose.

Banishing: cedar, clove, patchouli, or rose.

Binding: apple, cypress, dragon's blood (a resin), or pine.

Blessing: carnation, cypress, frankincense, lotus, or rosemary.

Changes: dragon's blood or peppermint.

Contacting the astral plane: frankincense.

Creativity: honeysuckle, lilac, lotus, or rose.

Determination: dragon's blood, musk, or rosemary.

Divination: cinnamon, honeysuckle, lilac, nutmeg, rose, or yarrow.

Energy, positive: bay, carnation, cinnamon, dragon's blood, frankincense, ginger, lotus, pine, or rosemary.

Exorcism: bay, cedar, frankincense, lavender, myrrh, pine, or yarrow.

Good luck: bayberry, cedar, or cinnamon.

Happiness or harmony: basil, cedar, clove, cypress, fir, gardenia, jasmine, lavender, lotus, myrrh, orange, patchouli, rose, or ylang-ylang.

Healing: carnation, cinnamon, clove, gardenia, lavender, lotus, orange, peppermint, or sandalwood.

Inspiration: acacia, clove, fir, lily of the valley, rosemary, or sage.

Love: amber, frangipani, gardenia, honeysuckle, jasmine, lavender, musk, patchouli, rose, vanilla, or ylang-ylang.

Meditation: acacia, bay, cinnamon, frankincense, jasmine, myrrh, or wisteria.

Prosperity: bayberry, bergamot, cinnamon, honeysuckle, jasmine, or vetiver.

Protection: bay, bayberry, cinnamon, dragon's blood, frankincense, jasmine, juniper, lotus, patchouli, pine, rosemary, sandalwood, or vervain.

Psychic abilities: ambergris, honeysuckle, lemon, lotus, mimosa, or wisteria.

Purification: bay, cedar, cinnamon, dragon's blood, frankincense, myrrh, peppermint, pine, rosemary, sage, or vervain.

Removal of hexes: cedar, myrrh, or vetiver.

Spirituality, increasing: frankincense, lotus, myrrh, or sandalwood.

Success: ginger.

Visions, spiritual: bay, frankincense, or lotus.

Willpower: rosemary.

Essential Oils

Oils are primarily used in candle-burning spells. To attract what you want, you rub the appropriate oil on the candle from the wick to the bottom. To rid yourself of something, you rub the oil on the candle from the bottom to the wick. If you wish, you may then roll the candle in the corresponding, crushed herbs.

You can also blend several drops of different oils together in a small vial to make your own personal oil of protection, love, prosperity, or whatever is needed for spells. Carefully label each bottle. If you wish, you can add a similar amount of cold-pressed almond oil to the essential oils to make the mixture go further.

Essential oils can be found in New Age shops in your town or online. Some of the "kitchen" oils can be purchased in cooking stores. Note: Be careful when oils come in contact with the skin—some people have allergic reactions and some oils can burn. Consult your herbal practitioner before using an oil with which you are not familiar.

Amber: happiness or love.

Bayberry: prosperity, protection, controlling a situation.

Bergamot: money or optimism.

Carnation: healing, energy, or protection.

Cedar: purification, healing, removal of hexes.

Cinnamon: money, purification, or energy.

Clove: healing or stimulating energy.

Dragon's blood: protection, purification, exorcism, or removing hexes.

Frangipani: love or to attract the perfect mate.

Frankincense: purification, protection, or to increase spirituality.

Frankincense and myrrh: protection, purification, or healing.

Gardenia: love, healing, harmony, or happiness.

Heliotrope: protection or attracting wealth.

Honeysuckle: money or to strengthen psychic abilities.

Jasmine: love, money, or to bring psychic dreams.

Juniper: protection.

Lavender: healing or love.

Lilac: protection.

Lotus: purification, protection, or to attract spiritual teachers.

Magnolia: becoming one with nature.

Musk: sexual love, attracting the opposite sex, or prosperity.

Myrrh: aid psychic development, healing, protection, or to break hexes.

Patchouli: purification, protection, or love.

Peppermint: stimulate creativity, energy, or attract money.

Pine: strength, protection, or purification.

Rose: love, fertility, or to cleanse the vibrations in a room or house.

Rosemary: protection.

Sage: purification or discovering the truth.

Sandalwood: cleansing or increasing spirituality.

Vanilla: sexual love or cleansing the mind for mental work.

Vetiver: money, love, or to remove hexes.

Violet: luck, love, or to find a solution to a problem.

Wisteria: to learn of and understand past lives.

Yarrow: exorcism or courage.

Ylang-Ylang: love or harmony.

Stones by Color

There are many books on the market that detail the meanings of each kind of stone. The lists are long, often involved, and frequently differ. The following list simply divides the stones into color categories to be used in magick. You should determine the meaning of each color in multicolored stones, so that you are not using a hue that works against your magick.

At the end of the list, I have included four distinct stones by name. These have very strong, specific powers that will double the powers in the other stones you use.

Black: Most people associate the color black with dark magick, however, it is more commonly used to repel hexes and curses or transform the dark energy into positive power. It also can be used to bind troublesome people or to release yourself from being bound. It is useful as a good all-round general defense.

Blue: This hue has been traditionally used for harmony and healing. It is also useful for gaining understanding or considering journeys and moves.

Brown: This color is especially good for attracting Earth Elementals. However, it will also amplify all Earth magick and any psychic abilities. Use it, too, for common sense and success.

Green: This is another hue for attracting Earth Elementals, particularly faeries and elves. Use it also for marriage, relationships, creativity, balance in your life, fertility, or money.

Indigo: This color in stones is extremely powerful. Use it to discover past lives, balance out karma, or understand your role in karmic problems. It is also helpful in stopping bad habits or experiences.

Orange: Use to change your luck, gain power, or get control of a situation.

Pink: Useful in finding pure love, friendship, or healing.

Purple: This color stone must be used carefully because it is so powerful. Add it to spells to break bad luck, gain success in long-term goals, grow in the psychic and spirit, or for protection.

Red: Use this color of stone for energy and taking action. It is also valuable in spells for courage to face a conflict or test.

White: White will help you to get past all illusions and get to the truth of any situation and aid you in staying centered and calm. It will also help to attract spiritual guidance or direct you into the right path.

Yellow: This stone increases mental powers, sparks creativity, or creates sudden changes.

Herbs

If you use herbs in homemade incenses or to coat an oiled candle, you must first grind them into a powder with a mortar and pestle. The modern equivalent of the mortar and pestle is a small electric coffee grinder. Whichever you use, keep the equipment for magickal use alone. Do not use it for ordinary household activities. Whole, slightly crushed, or powdered herbs may also be sprinkled in a circle around a candle.

Some of the following herbs can be found in the spice section of any grocery store or cooking outlet. You can gather and dry some of them yourself. Others you can purchase in New Age or Pagan shops.

Do not ingest any herb without knowing the reaction of that herb upon the body. Some herbs can produce a deadly effect.

Basil: protection or exorcism.

Bay laurel: stop interference from others or protect against evil.

Catnip: for love, happiness, or courage.

Chamomile: gain luck in gambling or get a marriage proposal.

Clove: friendship, banish evil, or gain a desire.

Dandelion: purification or to aid clairvoyance.

Dragon's blood: attracts good luck, protection, money, or love. Also removes hexes and curses.

Frankincense: purification, exorcism, raise spiritual vibrations, or protect.

Ginger: success, power, love, or money.

Jasmine flowers: attracts love, strengthens psychic abilities, or helps to gain money.

Juniper berries: protects against thieves or helps in developing your psychic gifts.

Lavender: attracts helpful spirits, useful to gain love or money.

Lemon verbena: very good for driving away evil or repelling unwanted lovers.

Lily of the valley: **do not eat** as this plant is *poisonous*. It is safer to use its oil to gain peace and knowledge.

Marigold: also known as calendula and pot marigold, used to have clairvoyant dreams.

Marjoram: also called sweet marjoram and pot marjoram, used for protection and purification.

Mugwort: helps strengthen the energies of divination, especially scrying devices, and protects.

Nutmeg: purification, protection, or increasing spirituality.

Orris root: will aid in divination or attract the opposite sex.

Patchouli: will break up any spell sent against you and is helpful in defeating enemies. It will also bring back a lost love or attract money.

Peppermint: purification, energy, love, or to increase psychic ability.

Pine: protection and purification.

Rose petals: love and happiness.

Rosemary: healing or exorcism. Will also keep a lover faithful.

Rue: defends against spells and dark magick. Purification, exorcism, repels negativity, or gets things moving, will also attract the right love for you.

Sage: purification, protection, or gaining wisdom.

St. John's Wort: healing, happiness, courage, love, protection, or helps with divination.

Sandalwood, red: healing, exorcism, protection, or gaining a wish.

Sandalwood, yellow: protection, exorcism, and strengthening spirituality.

Thyme: also called common thyme, creeping thyme, and Mother of thyme, it is used in healing, cleanses the aura, and cures nightmares.

Vervain: also known as holy herb and verbena, it repels psychic attacks and black magick. Purification, love, or attracting wealth.

Wormwood: repels black magick, removes hexes, and helps with developing the psychic areas of your life.

Yarrow: helps with divination and love spells, and has the power to keep couples happily married.

Index

Other Reading Sources

Conway, D. J. *The Ancient & Shining Ones*. St. Paul, Minn.: Llewellyn Publications, 1993.

———. *The Ancient Art of Faery Magick*. Berkeley, Calif. Ten Speed Press, 2005.

———. *Magickal Mermaids and Water Creatures*. Franklin Lakes, N.J.: New Page Books, 2005.

Cunningham, David Michael. *Creating Magickal Entities*. Perrysburg, Ohio: Egregore Publishing, 2003.

Cunningham, Scott. *Earth, Air, Fire & Water*. St. Paul, Minn.: Llewellyn Publications, 1992.

Johnson, Cait. *Earth, Water, Fire, & Air*. Woodstock, Vt.: Skylight Paths Publishing, 2003.

Lipp, Deborah. *The Elements of Ritual*. St. Paul. Minn.: Llewellyn Publications, 2003.

———. *The Way of Four*. St. Paul, Minn.: Llewellyn Publications, 2004.

McArthur, Margie. *Wisdom of the Elements*. Freedom, Calif.:The Crossing Press, 1998.

Pogacnik, Marko. *Nature Spirits & Elemental Beings*. Scotland, UK: Findhorn Press, 2004.

Pogacnik, Marko. *Healing the Heart of the Earth.* Scotland, UK: Findhorn Press, 1998.

Wolfe, Amber. *Druid Power*. St. Paul, Minn.: Llewellyn Publications, 2004.

—————. *Elemental Power*. St. Paul, Minn.: Llewellyn Publications, 1997.

Reading on Crop Circles

Andrews, Colin. *Crop Circles: Signs of Contact.* Franklin Lakes, N.J.: New Page Books, 2003.

Bartholomew, Alick, ed. *Crop Circles—Harbingers of World Change*. Baht, UK: Gateway Books, 1991.

Haselhoff, Eltjo. *The Deepening Complexity of Crop Circles*. Berkeley, Calif.: Frog, Ltd., 2001.

Hein, Simeon. *Opening Minds*. Boulder, Colo.: Mount Baldy Press, 2002.

Moore, Judith and Barbara Lamb. *Crop Circles Revealed*. Flagstaff, Ariz.: Light Technology Publishing, 2001.

Noyes, Ralph, ed. *The Crop Circle Enigma*. Bath, UK: Gateway Books, 1990.

Silva, Freddy. *Secrets in the Fields*. Charlottesville, Va.: Hampton Roads Publishing, 2002.

Thomas, Andy. *Vital Signs*. Berkeley, Calif.: Frog, Ltd., 2002.

About the AuthoR

A resident of the Pacific Northwest, **D. J. Conway** has spent more than 40 years studying and practicing Shamanism, New Age religions, Eastern philosophy, Wicca, and Paganism. A best-selling author of 27 books in these fields, her books have been translated into several foreign languages.

Ms. Conway is an honorary member of the Council of Elders of the Society of Celtic Shamans. She lives a quiet, private life with her cats and family. She can be reached through her Website at *www.djconway.com*.